Index

Holly Hill Apple Pie	44
How to make a really smooth soup or purée	143
How to steam a pudding	142
How to test that a cake or pudding is cooked	143
Huntingdon Fidget Pie	28
Loin of Pork with Apples	36
Mincemeat	128
Muesli	134
Normandy Apple Batter	77
Normandy Pheasant	26
Nutty Apple Stuffing	120
Oat Apple Pudding	69
Oat Crisp	138
Orient Pudding	81
Pommes a la Parisienne	83
Ripon Apple Pie	38
Saint Stephen's Pudding	57
Salmon and Apple Stew	39
Savoury Stuffed Apples	33
Spanish Apple Fritters	72
Spice Apple Pie	43
Spiced Apple Butter	125
Spiced Apple Cheesecake	104
Spicy Apple Soup	15
Suet Pastry	142
Swedish Apple Charlotte	66
Sweet-Sour Red Cabbage	114
Swiss Apple Gratin	85
Tarte aux pommes à l'alsacienne	101
Tarte Tatin	49
Tree Care	145
Toffee Apple Pudding	54
Toffee Apples	137
Twelfth Night Pie	34
Vanilla Sugar	143
Waldorf Salad	16
Witches Foam	79
Yoghurt and Apple Dressing	122
York Ham Cooked with Apples	35

Cooking Apples

This book of recipes found its inspiration
in the Orchards of Ampleforth Abbey;
many have contributed to its making.

EAN 978-0-9558357-1-1

Cooking Apples

by a monk of Ampleforth Abbey

Revised edition 2013

Published by Ampleforth Abbey Trust

Registered Charity No: 1026493

with a grant from the

Howardian Hills AONB Sustainable Development Fund

Printed by

Weblinks

Contents

Preface   5

Introduction   7

Soups & Salads   11

Main Courses   25

Desserts   41

Cakes & Baking   99

Miscellaneous   113

Tips & Tricks   141

Index   149

The "frosted" Grange

Preface

Almost 30 years ago Fr. Edmund Hatton and the late Caroline Miles published "Cooking Apples", a little collection of recipes revolving all around apples. Many of these had been suggested by kind visitors to the orchard at Ampleforth Abbey.

The book was aimed at helping people to get even more enjoyment from the delicious apples. It certainly must have achieved this because after a very short time it became a sought after rarity.

This new edition pursues the same aim but, since times have changed, it would like to go just a little bit further.

Enjoying apples and apple products in all their various forms and guises is enjoying a bit of nature. It seems that unfortunately our fast living times have separated us to a certain extend from the joyful experience of nature in general. This is quite a pity since particularly in this part of the North Ridings we have so much offered to us on the moors, down the dales and in the Howardian hills (which not without reason are classed as an Area of Outstanding Natural Beauty).

By including some images of the beautiful valley around Ampleforth Abbey I would like to nurture a little hope that they, together with the mouth-watering recipes might entice you to explore our area. The first step might be just out of the back door into the garden (perhaps the little chapter at the end about basic tree care might come in handy there); or it might be a visit to a local orchard (such as the Community Orchard at Gilling village). Or you might go on an exploration along the path and bridle-ways. What ever form it takes, it will have made worthwhile the effort of all those who have helped to put this book together.

A monk of Ampleforth Abbey
Feast of the Annunciation, 25th March 2009

The cookers start to bloom

Introduction

There are no exact records of what the monks did with regard to the provision of food when they arrived in the valley near Ampleforth at the beginning of the 19th century. They were a small but growing community who, from the very start, had an increasing number of pupils to look after in their growing school. The house they moved into had a garden and soon farms were acquired in the valley. A comparison with farms and holdings of that time suggests that apples would have played an important role by providing fresh nutritious fruit and vitamins during a good part of the year from early on.

Around 100 years later Abbot Smith planted the first orchard proper, of which only two trees remain today: a Lord Derby in front of the Procurator's building and a Keswick in the Second Master's garden. The small orchard soon grew along the road to Oswaldkirk and onto Aumit hill. There were changes in size and composition reflecting the ever growing need for fresh fruit by pupils and community alike.

One way of achieving larger yields combined with greater ease of picking and improved quality was the introduction of the East Malling row system by Fr. Edmund Hatton. His father, Sir Ronald Hatton, was for many years the director of the East Malling Research Station in Kent, where the system of spindle shaped dwarf apple trees was developed. The trees are planted in rows just enough apart to allow easy ground care and picking. Their height is checked so that the apples can be picked easily without any need for ladders, making the harvest cheaper, quicker and much safer. This way of growing apples allowed the rapid increase of table fruit production in the post-war years, but it relies very heavily on manual labour. Not only has all the picking to be done by hand, but the trees, growing so close together, need constant care all year round. Pruning is important to prevent them growing too high, and to maintain their shape. So also is pest control, and careful nutrition, since with small trees there is less margin for error. Where there are many similar trees so close

7

together, pests and diseases can spread very quickly and have devastating consequences.

To provide apples for the best part of the year, one cannot rely on producing a large amount of one particular apple and hope to store it for the rest of the season. Rather it is necessary to grow a number of varieties fruiting in succession. By choosing the right varieties, the Ampleforth monks created an orchard that supplies fresh apples from early August up to Christmas. The later varieties can even be stored in an aerated shed until well after Easter without the need for artificial cooling or gas-proof chambers.

Monks, orchard workers and students of the school have all helped over the years to tend the orchard and to pick the fruit, helping to increase production so much, that apples could be supplied to the surrounding villages and sold at the gate.

With the advent of cheap tinned and frozen processed apples, orchards all over the North had to adapt. Sunny days and cool nights are what helps the apples to develop their flavour, and in Yorkshire there is plenty of all that. Without the use of sprays and chemicals, apples at the Ampleforth Abbey Orchard are now grown mainly for their flavour as well as for their beauty. Those that can make it onto the table are sold either at the gate or to markets, restaurants and shops. The apples that are too small, deformed or have blemishes are first transformed into cider and then later into cider brandy and apple liqueur. In this way fragrance and flavour are preserved throughout the year.

The "Apple Season" lasts from summer to Easter producing many different varieties of different tastes and colours. A walk through the beautiful countryside of the Howardian Hills or the moors will with all probability lead you past small farms with apple trees in their gardens and orchards. (Who knows, with a bit of luck you may be able to convince the farmer or his wife to part with some of their fruit for you to have a taste?)

The early varieties in particular need to be eaten fresh; just off the tree is best for an Irish Peach or a Vista Bella.

As autumn approaches, though, there are apples with a more mature, stronger flavour, not so reliant on fragrance. Varieties such as Katy, Lord Lambourne, James Grieve and Red Gravenstein present a refreshing balance of sweetness and acidity together with an exciting crunch that make them interesting and enjoyable to eat. They do, together with the later varieties, have other uses too. First of all they make excellent juice. But they are also very welcome in the kitchen.

At the beginning of the harvesting season, in late August for instance, when the early Grenadier produces a deliciously light and fluffy smooth apple sauce, a coarsely grated Gravenstein serves to create a refreshing Waldorf Salad, or a firm James Grieve lends itself to a French Apple Tart.

Later, at the beginning of October, when the Grenadier (if kept on the tree) has developed more sweetness and its own flavour, it will happily lend itself to baking.

Salads, tarts and cakes, where fine flavour is the main concern will in general benefit from apples that are not usually referred to as cooking apples. (The distinction is rather artificial and, in my opinion, aimed mainly at the production of large amounts of apple sauce, stewed apple and apple pie). Blenheim Orange, Orleans Reinette, Belle de Boskoop and Crispin are all useful for making fine bakery and chutneys or jams when just ripe; after having been in storage for a while they not only increase in sweetness but are also enhanced in flavour. They will become excellent eaters late in the season and the New Year.

Even if there are no local apples available it is still possible to enjoy their fragrance and flavour: refreshing yourself in the summer's midday heat with a cider sorbet perhaps, or later in the evening savouring an after dinner tipple of cider brandy.

Lane's Prince Albert in bloom

Soups & Salads

"But by the red cheek never be misled:
For virtue, flavour, seek the acid green.
Of looks less kindly, but of sharp reward
Like stringent wit that keeps a matter keen"

V. Sackville West

Apple Soup

1½ lb cooking apples

water

brown sugar

1½ oz butter

1½ oz flour

½ pt milk

½ pt water or light stock

salt & pepper

Peel, core and coarsely chop the apples. Put into a heavy pan with a tablespoon of water and cook until soft, stirring occasionally to prevent burning. Add some sugar if needed.

Make a white sauce in the usual way. If you have a light chicken or veal stock available it may be used instead of the water, but do not use a stock cube; the flavour is too strong.

Liquidize together with the apples, dilute to soup consistency if necessary and check seasoning.

Serve hot.

Apple and Chestnut Soup

1 lb chestnuts in their shells

1 stick celery

2 large dessert apples (Orleans Reinette, Ingrid Marie or Ribston Pippin) peeled, cored and sliced

2 oz butter

3 pt light stock or water

4 oz single cream

salt & pepper

Prepare the chestnuts in the usual way.

(If you can't get chestnuts in their shells, or you haven't got time to prepare them, ½ lb pre-peeled vacuumed chestnuts or a tin of chestnuts in water make perfectly good substitutes. In this case you won't need to cook them for very long).

Cook the chestnuts in half the stock, with the chopped celery, for about 20 minutes, or until the nuts are quite soft.

Meanwhile simmer the apple slices in the butter with a little salt and pepper. When both chestnuts and apples are soft, liquidize together and dilute to soup consistency. Check the seasoning, and just before serving add the cream and stir. Serve with fried croutons.

Cucumber and Apple Soup

2 large cucumbers

1 lb cooking apples

1 lemon

1 small clove garlic, crushed

1 glass dry white wine

salt & pepper

sour cream or natural yoghurt

Peel, core and slice the apples. Cook them gently in a very little water with the juice and grated rind of the lemon. Blend roughly with hand blender or food processor.

Put the apple purée into a large bowl. Cut the cucumber in half and remove the seeds by running a teaspoon along its centre. Grate the peeled cucumbers into the apple purée. Sprinkle the mixture with salt and leave for at least two hours.

Add crushed garlic and wine, stir well and check the seasoning. A little fresh chopped dill or fennel makes a nice addition.

Chill well and serve topped with a swirl of sour cream or a spoonful of yoghurt in each bowl.

Spicy Apple Soup (A heart warming soup for a cold autumn night) *For 4 Portions*

4 apples (Crispin, Jester or Suntan)

2 medium sized red chillies

1 red pepper

1 clove of garlic

1 small cucumber

1 Tbsp butter

¾ l stock (vegetable stock to make it a vegetarian dish)

salt & pepper

½ tsp paprika powder (hot)

sugar

cider vinegar

100 g cream

Peel, core and coarsely chop the apples. Peel the cucumber, remove the seeds and chop. Halve the red pepper and remove the seeds. Cut 2 dozen very fine strips (used later as decoration). Coarsely chop the rest. Peel the garlic and squash with a strong fork or knife. Halve the chillies lengthwise and remove the seeds.

Briefly fry the garlic together with the apples and the chillies in hot butter, add the pepper and cucumber pieces and fry a few more minutes stir in the paprika powder. Add some of the stock and cook until all ingredients are soft. Gradually add the remaining stock.

Drive all through a sieve or use a hand blender. Season with the salt and pepper, sugar and cider vinegar. Finally stir in the cream.

Serve individually decorated with the thin pepper strips very briefly fried in some hot butter. Best accompanied by a crispy white bread roll.

Waldorf Salad

6 tart red apples (Ingrid Marie or Idared)

2 Tbsp lemon juice

3 sticks sliced celery

3 oz coarsely chopped walnuts

3 Tbsp mayonnaise or salad dressing

1 medium sized lettuce

Wash the apples. Quarter, core and dice coarsely without peeling. Toss in lemon juice.

Add celery, nuts and coat well with the mayonnaise or salad dressing.

Serve on crisp lettuce.

Apple and Nut Salad

3 crisp eating apples (Worcester Pearmain, Lord Lambourne, or Katy)

3 Tbsp lemon juice

2 oz shelled walnuts

¼ pt soured cream

2 oz red cabbage

2 sticks celery

8 large radishes

2 oz seedless raisins

salt & pepper

4 lettuce leaves

Wash apples and cut into medium sized chunks. Toss in lemon juice.

Chop walnuts, reserving a few for garnishing.

Pour cream into a bowl and stir in the apples and nuts.

Shred cabbage finely, slice the celery and radishes. Stir all into the cream mixture and season well. Serve on lettuce leaves and garnish with walnuts.

Apple and Raisin Slaw

1 lb white cabbage

1 small onion

4 oz carrots

¼ pt mayonnaise

1 dessert apple

lemon juice

2 Tbsp seedless raisins

salt & pepper

Discard outer cabbage leaves. Wash and thoroughly dry the cabbage and shred finely.

Finely chop the onion and grate or shred the carrots.

Core and chop the apple into 1 cm cubes (alternatively grate coarsely) and toss in lemon juice.

Add to the slaw with the raisins. Mix well.

Beetroot and Apple Salad

1 kg beetroot
1 kg apples (eg. Lord Lambourne or Kent)
1 onion
salt & pepper
juice of one lemon
sunflower oil

Bake the unpeeled beetroot gently in the oven until they are soft (45' – 50' at medium temperature). Top and tail. The skin can now easily be removed just with your fingers.

Dice the beetroot in 1 cm cubes.

Peel and quarter the apples. Cut out the cores. Dice like the beetroot.

Chop the onion finely.

Mix beetroot, apples and onion thoroughly. Add lemon juice, salt and pepper to taste (keeping in mind that some will be absorbed by the beetroot later). Mix again, add oil and mix for a last time.

Cover and store in the fridge.

You can use it freshly made, but it tastes better the next day.

Apple, Celery and Turkey Salad

equal weights of dessert apples - Cox or Reinette

celery

cold cooked turkey

3 oz gruyere for each ½ lb meat

vinaigrette dressing or

mayonnaise thinned with a little single cream

Core but do not peel the apples and cut them into dice. Slice the celery, and dice the meat. Cut the cheese into short match sticks. Mix all the ingredients together and pour over a vinaigrette dressing made with white wine or cider vinegar, a light olive oil or sunflower oil, salt, black pepper and a little mustard.

If watercress is available, serve the salad in a bowl lined with it. If not, sprinkle chopped parsley generously over the top.

A light and refreshing meal for one of the days after Christmas.

Bacon and Apple Salad

8 oz crumbled fried bacon

¼ pt diced apple

¼ pt sliced celery or radish

4 Tbsp mayonnaise

4 lettuce cups or watercress

Combine bacon, apple, celery and mayonnaise. If necessary, sprinkle with lemon or orange juice.

Fill lettuce cups or serve on a bed of watercress.

Cheese and Apple Salad

For 6 Portions

½ pt chopped red-skinned apple

2 oz cheddar cheese, cut in ½" cubes

4 Tbsp mayonnaise

1 tsp caster sugar

6 lettuce cups

½ pt sliced celery

¼ pt diced pineapple

3 Tbsp lemon juice

¼ tsp salt

Combine the apple, celery, cheese and pineapple. Stir the mayonnaise, lemon juice, sugar, and salt together until smooth. Pour over apple mixture and stir until well coated. Chill.

To serve, spoon into crisp lettuce cups.

Australian Summer Salad

4 sticks celery
⅓ cucumber
2 dessert apples
1 small lettuce
juice of one orange

Dice celery and cucumber.

Core apples, dice and add to celery and cucumber.

Toss well in orange juice. Chill for one hour.

Wash the lettuce and dry thoroughly. Crisp in the fridge.

Serve the salad on a bed of lettuce leaves.

Crimson Bramley at harvest time

Main Courses

*"Cooking is one of those arts which most requires
to be done by persons of religious nature"*

A.N. Whitehead

Normandy Pheasant

2 pheasants

6 large dessert apples (Sunset, Greensleeve or Ribston Pippin)

5 oz butter

4 oz double cream

salt & pepper

cinnamon

Brown the pheasants in half the butter. Peel, core and slice the apples; fry them lightly in the rest of the butter, sprinkling them with cinnamon as they cook. Put a thin layer of cooked apples into a deep casserole, arrange the pheasant on top, breast down, and tuck the rest of the apples round the bird so that it is embedded in them. Pour in half the cream. Cover and cook in an oven, gas Mark 4/180°C, for about an hour, turning the bird breast side up at half time and seasoning it with salt and pepper. Remove the pheasant from the casserole, add the rest of the cream to the apple mixture and allow to heat through. Carve the bird and serve surrounded by the savoury apple gravy.

Keep the accompaniments simple - game chips and a watercress salad.

Escalopes of Veal with Apple

4 escalopes of veal

1 large or 2 small dessert apples (Sunset, Idared or Jupiter)

4 oz double cream

butter

seasoning

cider brandy

Peel and core the apples and cut into small cubes. Melt some butter in a heavy frying pan and brown the escalopes quickly on both sides. Add the apple cubes and cook for 2 or 3 minutes. Warm a small liqueur glass of cider brandy in a little pan, set light to it and pour over the meat and apple cubes, shaking the pan until the flames die down. Transfer the meat to a warm dish, add the cream to the apple and juices in the pan and stir to heat through, scraping up all the delicious brown bits from the bottom of the pan. Season with salt and pepper. Arrange the cubes of apple on top of the escalopes, pour the sauce round, and serve at once.

Huntingdon Fidget Pie

1 lb cooking apples
½ lb onions
¼ lb streaky home-cured bacon
seasoning
8 oz shortcrust or flaky pastry

Peel, core and slice the apples. Cut the onions into rings. Dice the bacon.

Put a layer of apple in the bottom of a large pie dish, then a layer of onion and finally a layer of bacon. Sprinkle with salt and pepper. Repeat until the dish is full.

Pour on about ½ pint of water and cover with a pastry crust.

Bake at Mark 3/170°C for 2 hours. Brush the pastry with milk and return to a hot oven Mark 7/220°C, for 10 minutes to brown the top.

Himmel und Erde

1 kg large (soft cooking) potatoes

1 kg strong flavoured apples (e.g. Lanes Prince Albert, Lord Derby, Belle de Boskoop or Cockpit)

2 large onions

200 g smoked streaky bacon

4 slices of black pudding

sugar

butter

salt & pepper

Peel potatoes and cut into large chunks (as for boiled potatoes). Cook with about 2 teaspoons of salt until tender.

Meanwhile peel, core and quarter the apples. Simmer gently with a tablespoon of sugar (or more if needed) and a little water until soft. When the potatoes are ready, drain off most of the water and mash them coarsely. Add the apples with their juices and stir a bit until the apples start to disintegrate but before they blend in completely. Keep warm.

Peel and finely slice the onions and dice the bacon. Melt the butter and saute the onions and bacon.

Fry the black pudding in some butter.

Portion out the potatoes place a slice of black pudding on top and spoon over onions, bacon and liquid butter.

Grilled Pork Chops with Cider Sauce

4 pork chops
3 - 4 shallots
salt & pepper
parsley
glass of cider

Chop shallots and parsley very finely and season with salt and pepper. Moisten the chops with a little oil or melted butter and spread half the mixture over them.

Grill for 10 minutes or longer, depending on the thickness of the chops. Turn the chops, spread the rest of the shallot mixture over their other sides and grill until cooked.

Transfer the chops to a serving dish, and loosen juices and bits in the pan with a glass of cider. Reduce the sauce until it is quite thick.

Pour over the chops and serve.

Fried Apple and Cheese Sandwich

For 4 Portions

2 howgate wonder apples (or 3 large Crispin apples)

2 oz butter

sliced cheese to cover

8 slices sandwich loaf

butter or oil for frying

Peel and core the apples. Cut each into 4 thick slices and fry lightly in butter, turning once. Keep warm in oven. Remove crusts from bread. Spread with butter on one side and cover with a slice of cheese. Sandwich in pairs with a slice of apple in the centre. Press firmly together and fry in shallow fat until golden and crisp (both sides).

Top each sandwich with a fried apple slice and serve immediately.

Gammon with Marmalade and Apple Glaze

Gammon joint
4 oz marmalade (thick)
2 dessert apples
lemon juice

In a large pot simmer joint in plenty of water for half the cooking time (about 30 minutes per kg).

Strip off skin and bake at gas Mark 4/180°C until 20 minutes before end of cooking time. Meanwhile peel, core and slice apples and dip the slices in lemon juice. Warm the marmalade. Brush gammon joint liberally with marmalade and arrange the apple slices over the fat. Secure them with wooden cocktail sticks and brush remainder of marmalade over them. Increase oven heat to gas Mark 7/220°C and bake for 20 minutes, basting frequently.

Savoury Stuffed Apples

6 large cooking apples (Rev. Wilkes, Howgate Wonder or Lord Derby)

2 oz butter

1 tsp soy sauce

4 shallots

2 oz seedless raisins

½ lb pork fillet

juice of a lemon

1 clove of garlic (crushed)

4 oz demarara sugar

1 tsp mustard

1 glass of cider

salt & pepper

Melt the butter in a heavy saucepan, chop the shallots finely and cook for a few minutes. Cut the pork into ½ inch cubes and add to the shallots. Cook gently for 5 minutes. Add the garlic, mustard, soy sauce, raisins, lemon juice and sugar. Season well and add some of the cider. Cook the mixture gently for ½ hour, adding more cider from time to time.

When cooked core the apples, scoop out sufficient pulp from the centre to make a good cavity. Score the skin in the middle circumferentially. Stuff apples with the mixture, stand them in a baking tin containing a little water, cover with greased paper and bake at Mark 4/180°C for about 20 minutes. The cooking time depends upon the apples. (They should be just cooked through but not breaking up.)

Serve at once.

Twelfth Night Pie

6 oz lard

7 oz water (⅓ pt)

1 lb plain flour salt

2 lb chopped left over meats - turkey, goose, ham, sausages. Be sure to include some fat ham or bacon, particularly if you have a lot of turkey to use up

chopped herbs

salt & pepper

½ pt (approx) jellied gravy or stock add gelatine if necessary

½ lb cored, chopped, unpeeled apple

A raised pie, for which you need a hinged pie mould or a deep cake tin with a removable base.

To make the pastry, bring water and lard to the boil and tip the boiling mixture into the seasoned flour. Mix as rapidly as possible, and set aside until it is just cool enough to handle. It must not be allowed to get cold. Cut off about ¼ for the lid, and tip the rest into the greased, floured mould. Quickly and lightly shape the pastry up the sides of the mould, making sure there are no gaps or cracks.

Put in the meat, seasoned with herbs, pepper, and salt if needed. Cover with a layer of chopped apples, and pour in the warmed stock or gravy. Finally brush round the edges of the pastry case with beaten egg and stick the lid on firmly. Cut a hole for the steam to escape, and use the pastry trimmings to decorate the top. Brush with beaten egg.

Bake at Mark 6/200°C for 30 minutes, and at Mark 3/170°C for a further hour. If you have used any uncooked meat or bacon it may need rather longer.

York Ham Cooked with Apples

1 lightly smoked ham (approx. 14 lb)
1½ lb cooking apples
1 lb soft brown sugar
¾ pt cider vinegar
4 oz soft brown sugar
4 Tbsp french mustard

1½ Tbsp dry sherry

Soak ham for up to 24 hours, changing the water at least 3 times to remove the salt. Wash in cold water and scrub with a stiff brush. Put ham in a large pan of cold water and bring to the boil.

Peel and quarter the apples and add to the pan with the brown sugar and vinegar. Partially cover the pan and simmer for 18 minutes per pound. The ham should be covered by the water during cooking.

When the ham is cooked and cool enough to handle, remove the skin and excess fat.

Mix brown sugar, mustard and sherry into a paste. Spread all over the ham.

Bake for 40 minutes at Mark 4/180°C, basting occasionally with the juices.

Let cool, and serve thinly sliced.

Loin of Pork with Apples

2 loins of pork

salt & pepper

garlic

knob of butter

3 Tbsp olive oil

2 onions

caraway

3 Tbsp tomato puree

¼ l cider

2 apples (Belle de Boskoop, Ingrid Marie or Lord Derby)

parsley

flour

cider brandy

1 Tbsp arrowroot

double cream

Rub the pork loins with salt and pepper and crushed garlic. Flour lightly and brown all around in the mixture of butter and oil. Keep warm. Chop the onions and roast them in the residues left behind by the browned loins. Add the caraway and chopped parsley. Briefly roast the tomato purée. Now wash the font loose with cider. Return the meat to the saucepan and roast it in the pre-heated oven (180°C) for 10 minutes. Cut the apples into quarters, peel, core and cut into generous segments. Add these to the meat and continue to roast for another 5 minutes.

Carefully remove the meat and the apple segments from the pan, stir well loosening any font sticking to the bottom. Bring to the boil on the hob. Add a small quantity of cider brandy to the arrowroot, stirring carefully to avoid any lumps and whisk into the boiling gravy. Let it come up once and take off the boil. Add some double cream and some more cider brandy to taste. Slice the meat and decorate on a warmed plate with the apple segments.

Serve with potato and parsnip mash or potato gratin.

Apple Burger with a Curry Dip

3 slices dried white bread

1 apple (Idared, Spartan, Fiesta or Crispin)

1 onion

500 gr minced meat

1 egg

50 gr raisins

250 gr cream

1 Tbsp lemon juice

2 Tbsp curry powder

salt & pepper

knob of butter

olive oil

Steep the bread in some water for 2 hours.

Peel, core and finely chop the apple. Peel and finely chop the onion.

Drain the bread and press out as much water as possible (without losing all the bread).

Mix meat, egg, onion and bread thoroughly for at least 5 minutes, until it binds well.

Now add the apple and raisins.

Form 8 burgers.

Mix cream, lemon juice and curry powder and stir thoroughly, add salt and pepper to taste, creating a curry dip.

Heat up the butter and add enough oil to fry the burgers on both sides.

These burgers are delicious whether they are served warm or cold.

Ripon Apple Pie

1¼ lb cooking apples

2 oz wensleydale cheese

3 - 4 oz sugar

12 oz shortcrust pastry

Line a 9" pie plate or flan dish with pastry. Peel, core and slice the apples thinly, and arrange them in the dish, sprinkling them with sugar as you go. Top with the grated cheese, and cover with a pastry lid in the usual way. Bake for 30 minutes at Mark 6/200°C.

Salmon and Apple Stew

800 g salmon filet, skinned and coarsely cubed

salt & pepper

juice of 1 lemon

2 apples, peeled, cored and coarsely cubed

3 shallots, finely chopped

1 Tbsp butter

200 mls cream

1 bunch chopped chives

Season the salmon cubes with salt and pepper and the lemon juice. Mix through and let marinate for a little while.

Sweat the shallots ⅓ of the butter until golden, add the apple cubes to fry until just soft. Remove the apple sauce from the pan and keep warm.

Drain the salmon as you melt the butter in the pan. Fry briefly and then add the apple sauce. Sprinkle generously with chives.

Best served with rice or tagliatelle.

Winston - one of the late eating apples

Desserts

"Sir, we could not have had a better dinner
had there been a Synod of Cooks"

Samuel Johnson

Deep Dish Apple Pie

1½ lb cooking apples

3 - 4 oz sugar

water

8 oz shortcrust pastry

For this pie you need a deep dish of about 2 pint capacity, with a central support to hold up the crust.

Peel, core and chop the apples, not too finely. Pile them into the dish, sprinkling the sugar over them as you go. Add a little water, to come about ⅓ up the sides of the dish.

Roll out the pastry to a shape about 1" larger than the top of the dish. Cut off a strip about ¾" wide all round, brush with water and arrange round the rim of the dish, damp side down. Brush upper side with water and put on the lid, cutting a hole for the steam to escape through the centre. Press edges together firmly with the back of a fork. Brush the lid with milk or lightly beaten egg white, sprinkle on a thick layer of caster sugar, and bake for 20 minutes at mark 6/200°C, and a further 20 minutes at Mark 5/190°C.

Spice Apple Pie

1½ lb cooking apples   sugar

2 oz sultanas

2 oz brown sugar

grated rind and juice of 1 small orange

generous pinch ground cinnamon

8 oz puff pastry

Peel, core and chop the apples. Mix with sultanas, brown sugar, cinnamon and orange rind and put into the pie dish. Pour over the orange juice and cover with the pastry. Cut a small hole in the middle to let the steam out. Brush top with milk or egg white and sprinkle with sugar.

Bake 20 minutes at Mark 7/220°C, and a further 20 - 25 minutes at Mark 4/180°C.

Holly Hill Apple Pie (A hermit's dish)

1 lb cooking apples

1 - 2 oz sultanas

grated orange rind

3 - 4 oz sugar

1 oz butter

1 breakfast cup cake or breadcrumbs

1 tsp mixed spice

12 oz shortcrust pastry

Line a shallow pie dish with half the pastry.

Mix crumbs, spice, grated orange rind, sultanas and half the sugar, and add melted fat. Spread the mixture over the pastry, and cover with cored, but not peeled, chopped apples, sprinkling them with the rest of the sugar. Cover with the rest of the pastry, and bake at Mark 7/220°C for about ½ hour.

When they are available you can add blackberries or blackcurrants. In that case omit sultanas and orange rind, halve the weight of apples and substitute the remainder with the berries. Add a little extra sugar if they are very sharp.

Apple Mince Pie

1 lb cooking apples

4 oz mixed dried fruit - sultanas, currants, chopped dates, chopped peel - whatever you have

2 Tbsp golden syrup

generous pinch of mixed spice

12 oz shortcrust pastry

Peel, core and chop the apples, and mix with the dried fruit, spice, and warmed syrup.

Line a pie plate with half the pastry and put the apple mixture into it. Cover with a pastry lid and bake at Mark 6/200°C for 30 minutes.

Note if the dried fruit is very dry soak for ½ hour in cold water then drain and mix.

Garrion Apple Pie

4 large cooking apples

2 oz flour

2 oz medium cut oatmeal

3 oz butter

2 eggs

2 tsp sugar

little almond essence (optional)

apricot or plum jam

Cream butter and sugar. Add beaten egg and essence if used.

Sift the flour and add the oatmeal. Add this to the mixture.

Spread the soft paste evenly over the bottom of a shallow pie dish and a little up the sides.

Peel and core the apples and slice in segments like an orange. Arrange the slices in overlapping rows over the paste until it is covered.

Spread the jam over the top and bake for 30 minutes in a moderate oven (Mark 4/180°C).

Serve immediately.

French Apple Tart

1¼ lb eating apples (Orleans Reinette, Sunset or Kidd's Orangered)

1½ oz unsalted butter

1 Tbsp sugar

2 Tbsp apricot jam

8 oz shortcrust pastry

Line a 9" shallow pie dish (a china or pottery flute-edged flan dish is ideal) with the pastry. Peel, core and slice the apples and cook very gently in the butter until they are soft and transparent, but not mushy. Stir in sugar to taste - do not make them too sweet.

Remove apples from the pan with a slotted spoon and arrange them carefully on the pastry.

Bake for 25 - 30 minutes at Mark 6/200°C, until the pastry is brown and the apples browned on top.

While the tart is cooking, warm the apricot jam in the apple juices, diluting with a little water if necessary to make quite a thin sauce. Sieve and brush this sauce over the tart, sprinkle liberally with caster sugar and put the tart back into the oven for a couple of minutes, until the sugar is just bubbling.

Best eaten with cream warm or just cold, but not refrigerated.

Apple Streusel Pie

8 oz shortcrust pastry

6 dessert apples, preferably Cox or Reinette

grated rind and juice of 1 lemon

2 oz sugar

cinnamon and nutmeg or allspice

3 oz soft brown sugar

3 oz plain flour

sifted 3 oz butter

Line an 8 - 9" flan dish with the pastry and arrange on it the apples, peeled, cored, sliced and tossed in lemon juice. Mix sugar and spices, and sprinkle over the apples.

To make the topping, combine flour, sugar and the lemon rind. Soften the butter and cut it into this mixture until it is like coarse breadcrumbs. Sprinkle over the apples.

Bake at Mark 6/200°C for 15 minutes, reduce heat to mark 4/180°C and bake for a further 20 - 30 minutes.

Serve cold, with whipped cream.

Tarte Tatin

8 - 10 dessert apples (Orleans Reinette, Kent or Ribston Pippin)

150 g butter

150 g sugar

250 g shortcrust pastry

30 g sugar

50 g butter

Preheat your oven at Mark 4/180°C.

Grease a round deep oven-proof dish of 26 cm (preferably with sloping sides) and shake in 150 g sugar so that the sides are coated and most of the sugar forms an even bed.

Peel and cut the apples into six even segments. Cut out the cores. Place the apple segments tightly on top of the sugar in the dish. Fill in all gaps with smaller segments. When all apples are in the dish heat it briskly on the hob. Reduce the heat as soon as a light caramel is forming (check by sliding a knife-blade in on the side occasionally). Now place the dish in the oven for 15 minutes.

Meanwhile roll out the pastry large enough to cover the dish with a generous margin.

After the apples have cooked for 15 minutes take the dish out, sprinkle with 30 g sugar and the flaked 50 g butter. Cover with the pastry tucking in the sides. Pierce the pastry a few times with a fork and return to the oven. After a further 15 – 20 minutes (when the pastry is golden-brown) remove from the oven. Let cool for a few minutes and reverse carefully onto a bigger oven-proof dish, avoiding any splashes of melted caramel!

Serve hot. (The original dish is served without any cream, ice cream or custard).

Apple Strudel

500 g flour

¼ l water

2 eggs

pinch of salt

2 Tbsp oil

¼ l milk

1 Tbsp sugar

1.5 kg apples (Lanes Prince Albert, Belle de Boskoop or Orleans Reinette)

100 g sugar

80 g raisins

½ lemons juice

250 ml soured cream or double cream

140 g butter

Sieve the flour onto your working surface. Stir together water, eggs and salt. Add gradually to the flour until it is smooth. Sparsely oil and let rest for 30 minutes in a warm place.

Peel, core and chop the apples into 1 – 2 cm chunks, shaking them together with the lemon juice to avoid browning. Add raisins and cream. Preheat the oven at Mark 5/190°C. Melt the 80 g butter.

Divide the dough into 4 equal portions and roll them on a well floured surface into very thin oblongs the length of your baking tray. Transfer the dough sheets individually onto a smooth towel. Brush with melted butter and cover with a quarter of the apple filling. Leave a margin of 3 cm at the sides and of 10 cm at one of the long sides. Now fold over the long edge without the margin and gently, lifting up the towel, form the strudel into a roll.

Place milk, sugar and remaining melted butter in your baking tray and add your strudels. Break the 60 g butter into small flakes sprinkling them over the rolls.

Bake 45 minutes at 190 °C. Serve hot with cream or custard, or cold with whipped cream.

Dorset Apple Cake

225g butter

500g apples (Greensleeves, Jester, or Orleans Teinette)

1 lemon (for grated zest and juice)

225g sugar

3 eggs

225g flour

2½ tsp baking powder

25g ground almonds

1½ Tbsp Demerara sugar

butter

icing sugar

clotted or whipped cream

Preheat the oven to Mark 4/180°C. Butter a deep 26 cm springform cake pan, line the bottom with baking paper.

Peel, core and dice the apples into 1 cm pieces, toss in the lemon juice.

Cream butter and sugar in a bowl until light and fluffy, add lemon zest. Beat in the eggs, 1 at a time. Add ¾ of the flour in portions (avoiding lumps).

Mix the remaining flour with the baking powder and sift into the bowl. Fold in together with the ground almonds. Drain the apple pieces well, and fold into the dough.

Spoon into the prepared cake pan, levelling the top. Sprinkle generously with the brown sugar and bake for 1 hour.

Leave to cool in the tin for 10 minutes. Turn the cake out and remove baking paper from the bottom.

Place on a serving plate and dust with icing sugar. Serve warm with clotted or lightly whipped cream.

Eve's Pudding

500 g apples (e.g Bramley, Lanes Prince Albert)   50 g butter

2 Tbsp sugar   50 g sugar

grated lemon zest   1 egg

1 Tbsp water   1 Tbsp milk

icing sugar

100 g self raising flour

Peel, core and slice the apples and pack them into a well buttered pie dish.

Sprinkle with sugar and a little lemon zest. Spoon the water over the top.

Cream together butter and sugar. Beat in the egg and sift in the flour. Mix well.

Spoon the cake mixture over the apple slices and smooth over with a knife.

Bake at 190°C for 35 – 40 minutes

Dust with icing sugar and serve hot.

Apple Roly Poly

6 oz self-raising flour

3 oz shredded suet

1 egg

water to mix

1 lb cooking apples (Lord Derby, Belle de Boskoop or Crispin)

2 - 3 oz sugar

(If you haven't made suet pastry before, see in the Tips & Tricks section how to make the dough and how to steam it).

Make a suet pastry adding the egg before you add any water.

Roll out on a floured board as if for a Swiss roll. Spread with peeled, cored, finely chopped apples mixed with sugar. A few currants, grated lemon peel or spices to taste may be added. Roll up and seal, pinching the ends together firmly, and tie in a well floured smooth cotton cloth. Put the pudding into a large pan of fast-boiling water and boil for about 1½ hours.

When cooked, turn the pudding out onto a serving dish. Serve hot with custard.

Toffee Apple Pudding

1½ lb cooking apples (Bramley or Lord Derby)　　2 oz butter

6 Tbsp sugar　　2 oz brown sugar

8 oz self-raising flour

4 oz suet

¼ pt water

pinch of salt

Cream together the butter and brown sugar and spread thickly round the inside of a 2 pint pudding basin. Make a suet pastry and line the basin with it, keeping enough for a lid. Fill with the apples, peeled, cored and chopped, mixed with the rest of the sugar. Damp the edges of the pastry lining and fit on the lid.

Tie down with a cloth in the usual way and steam for 1½ hours. Alternatively, the pudding may be baked at Mark 4/180°C for about 1¼ hours, standing the basin in a dish of water. Or slow-cook on 'high' setting for 3½ - 4 hours.

Cousin Polly's Pudding

4 oz soft white breadcrumbs

2 oz shredded suet

2 oz sugar

2 oz currants

1 large or 2 small cooking apples, peeled, cored
and finely chopped

1 oz candied peel (or grated rind of 1 lemon)

2 eggs, well beaten

2 - 3 Tbsp milk

Mix all ingredients together, pile into a greased 1½ pint pudding basin, tie down in the usual way and steam for 2 hours, or cook in a slow cooker.

Apple Raisin Pudding

8 oz cooking apples

2 Tbsp water

12 oz self-raising flour

1 level tsp powdered cinnamon

½ level tsp mixed spice

4 Tbsp milk

3 oz butter

1 oz chopped walnuts

3 oz raisins

4 oz brown sugar

2 eggs

Peel, core and slice the apples and stew in the water. Cook, purée and sieve.

Sift together the flour, cinnamon, and mixed spice.

Rub in the butter, stir in the walnuts, raisins, and brown sugar. Mix well with the eggs and the apple purée. Mix to a soft dropping consistency with the milk. Put into a greased basin, cover and steam.

Saint Stephen's Pudding

4 oz fresh breadcrumbs

2 oz soft brown sugar

4 oz seedless raisins

2 medium sized cooking apples (Lord Derby,
Bramley or Belle de Boskoop)

grated rind of one lemon

2 oz sifted self-raising flour

3 oz suet

pinch of salt

1 egg

3 Tbsp milk

Combine all the dry ingredients in a large mixing bowl and add the raisins.

Peel, core and grate the apples and add them with the grated lemon rind to the mixture.

Beat the egg into the milk and stir into the pudding mixture.

Butter a 2 pint pudding basin and pour in the mixture. Cover with greaseproof paper and a pudding
cloth tied with string.

Steam for 2 hours and serve with custard or brandy butter.

Brown Betty

1 lb cooking apples

4 oz brown breadcrumbs

2 oz brown sugar

2 oz dried fruit (optional)

3 Tbsp golden syrup

½ tsp mixed spice rind

juice of one lemon

Peel, core and slice the apples finely. Butter a pie dish and put a layer of slices in the bottom. Cover with crumbs and sprinkle with sugar and spices.

Repeat these layers until the dish is full. Add the lemon juice and grate the rind on top.

Warm the syrup and pour over. Bake in a moderate oven, Mark 4/180°C, for 30 minutes.

(Alternatively, this recipe can be steamed in a pudding basin for 1½ - 2 hours).

Apple Roll

2½ cups peeled, chopped apples

½ tsp cinnamon

2 cups flour

pinch of salt

1 Tbsp & 1 tsp baking powder

2 cups syrup

juice of one lemon (optional)

6 Tbsp butter

½ cup water

Preheat oven to Mark 7/220°C. Heat syrup to boiling and keep hot in an 8" square tin. Make a pastry with flour, butter and other ingredients. Roll out dough in oblong to ⅓" thick (approx. 12" long, 6 - 8" wide).

Sprinkle apples, cinnamon and optional lemon over dough. Roll up and pinch edges to seal. Cut into slices about 1½" wide. Place slices, cut edge down into boiling syrup. Bake for 25 minutes, spoon syrup over the cakes and serve warm with cream.

Apple Oat Crumble

1 lb cooking apples

2 oz brown sugar

3 oz quick porridge oats

2 oz butter

1 oz brown sugar

1 Tbsp cornflour

Peel, core and slice the apples and put them in a baking dish, sprinkling with 2 oz sugar. Mix together oats, cornflour and the remaining ounce of sugar, and stir in the melted butter. Cover the apples with this mixture, patting it down firmly.

Bake at Mark 4/180°C for about 35 minutes, until the top is brown and the apples are soft. Serve with cream or custard.

Apple and Date Crumble

4 oz flour

2 oz butter

1½ lb apples (Lanes Prince Albert, Belle de Boskoop or Orleans Reinette)

2 oz dates

2 oz sugar

1 tsp cinnamon

Sift the flour into a mixing bowl and rub in the butter. Stir in the sugar.

Peel, core and slice the apples. Chop the dates. Place the fruit in a pie dish and spoon over 2 tablespoons of water and a little sugar.

Sprinkle the crumble over the top and bake for 20 minutes at Mark 5/190°C.

Serve with custard or cream.

Apple Charlotte

1½ lb cooking apples

3 - 4 oz brown sugar

7 - 8 slices of white bread

4 oz butter

These quantities should be enough to fill a 9" square baking tin (about 2" deep) or a rectangular dish of similar capacity.

Remove crusts from the bread and spread thickly on both sides with softened butter. Cut each slice into fingers and line the dish, keeping enough to cover the top. Press the fingers together and push the lining firmly against the sides of the dish. Fill with the apples, peeled, cored and sliced thinly, sprinkling them with sugar as you go. Keep 1 tablespoon of sugar for the top. When the dish is full, cover with the remainder of the bread and dust with sugar.

Bake at Mark 5/190°C until the bread is crisp and golden brown and the apples are soft, about 40 minutes. If the bread starts to burn before the apples are cooked reduce the heat.

There are many delicious variations on this pudding. Use a fruit loaf for the lining (you will probably not need so much sugar). Add grated lemon or orange rind and a little juice from whichever fruit you choose, or add a few sultanas. It is also very good with the lining spread with marmalade as well as butter - do this after you have put it into the dish if you don't want to land up with most of it on your fingers!

Apple Pan Dowdy

3 large cooking apples

2 level Tbsp brown sugar

1 level tsp golden syrup

¼ level tsp grated nutmeg

¼ level tsp ground cinnamon

4 Tbsp milk

4 oz self-raising flour

pinch of salt

1 egg

2 oz butter

2 oz sugar

Peel, core and thinly slice the apples. Put into a 7" greased cake tin with the brown sugar, syrup, nutmeg and cinnamon. Cover with foil and bake in a moderately hot oven (Mark 5/190°C) for 20 minutes. Sift the flour and salt into a bowl. Beat the egg and melt the butter. Add the sugar, egg, milk and butter to the flour and beat well together.

Spoon this mixture on top of the apples and spread evenly. Return to the oven and bake uncovered for a further 30 to 40 minutes.

Turn upside-down onto a serving dish.

Apple Almond Pudding

1½ lb cooking apples (Lord Derby, Rev. Wilkes or Belle de Boskoop)

2 oz soft brown sugar

4 oz butter

4 oz caster sugar

4 oz ground almonds

2 eggs

Peel, core and slice the apples and cook them with the brown sugar and a tablespoon of water until they are quite soft. Put the cooked apple in a buttered dish at least 2" deep.

Cream butter and caster sugar until light. Beat in the eggs one at a time, and finally fold in the ground almonds. Cover the apples with this mixture, spreading it evenly, and bake at Mark 4/180°C for about 40 minutes. The top should be golden brown. Best served warm, after it has been out of the oven for about ½ hour, which makes it a very useful pudding for parties.

Apple and Grape Clafoutis

2 dessert apples, peeled, cored and sliced (Lord Lambourne, Crispin or Ingid Marie)

4 oz grapes (the large spanish red ones, or muscats) halved and with the pips removed

2 oz flour

2 oz caster sugar

3 eggs

1 pt hot milk

1½ Tbsp cider brandy or armangnac

butter

vanilla sugar (see tips & tricks)

Butter a flan dish or cake pan and arrange the apple slices and grapes over the bottom of it.

To make the batter, beat together the eggs and sugar, stir in the flour, and then the hot milk, beating well with a wooden spoon. Stir in the Cider Brandy or Armagnac.

Pour the batter over the fruit and bake for 30 minutes at Mark 6/200°C, adding small cubes of butter to the top half way through the cooking time. Remove from the oven, sprinkle with vanilla sugar and serve warm, with or without cream.

Swedish Apple Charlotte

4 oz fresh white breadcrumbs

6 oz butter

4 oz sugar

2 lb cooking apples (Grenadier or Bramley)

2 oz sugar

grated lemon rind

2 oz grated chocolate

Melt the butter in a large frying pan and fry the breadcrumbs gently until they are golden and crisp. This will take about ¼ hour: it is important not to hurry them or they will burn. Stir in the sugar and leave to cool.

Peel, core and cut up the apples and stew them in 2 - 3 tablespoons of water until you have a thick soft purée. Add 2 oz sugar and lemon rind and cool.

Arrange alternate layers of apple and breadcrumbs in a 2 pint dish. A glass dish or bowl is nice if you have one. Finish off with a layer of breadcrumbs, cover with whipped cream and sprinkle the grated chocolate over the top. Chill well before serving.

For a hot version of this pudding, sprinkle the chocolate over the final layer of breadcrumbs and bake in a medium oven, Mark 4/175°C, for 20 - 25 minutes.

Danish Apple and Chocolate Pudding

1½ lb cooking apples

3 - 4 oz sugar

grated rind and juice of 1 lemon

6 oz fresh white breadcrumbs

3 oz unsalted butter

2 Tbsp cocoa

2 oz Demerara sugar

¼ pt cream, whipped

Peel, core and slice the apples and cook with sugar, lemon juice and rind, until you have a thick purée.

Leave to cool.

Melt the butter in a large heavy pan and fry the breadcrumbs in it until golden brown. The heat should be kept low or the crumbs will burn. The frying process will take about 15 minutes. Mix demerara sugar with cocoa and stir the mixture into the crumbs. Leave to cool.

Put a layer of apple purée in a fairly deep glass dish, then a layer of chocolate crumbs. Repeat the layers, and cover the top with whipped cream. Chill well before serving.

Grasmere Apple Gingerbread

For 8 Portions

2½ lb cooking apples

6 oz sugar

2 - 3 Tbsp water

grated rind and juice of a lemon

8 oz plain flour

1 tsp ground ginger

4 oz sugar

4 oz unsalted butter

pinch of bicarbonate of soda

Peel, core and slice the apples and cook with sugar and water and the lemon rind and juice to make a soft purée. When cold, spread evenly over a large flan dish (11 - 12" diameter) or a 2½ - 3 pint capacity pie dish.

To make the topping, sift together the flour, bicarbonate of soda, ginger and a small pinch of salt.

Rub in the softened butter until the mixture is like coarse breadcrumbs, and stir in the sugar. Sprinkle this mixture over the apples and smooth the top with a palette knife.

Bake for about 30 minutes at Mark 4/165°C. The crust should be a pale golden brown.

Serve cold, with cream or home-made vanilla ice cream.

68

Oat Apple Pudding

1 cooking apple (Howgate Wonder or Lord Derby)

1 cup rolled oats

1½ oz butter

2 Tbsp sugar

Melt the butter and fry the oats. When starting to brown stir in the sugar.

Do not over cook - mix well. Cool.

Cut up, or coarsely grate the apple - sprinkle with lemon juice.

Shortly before serving, mix oats and apple.

Serve with thick cream.

Apple Fritters

4 oz self-raising flour
(or plain flour & 1 tsp baking powder)
1 tsp sugar
salt
1 egg
¾ pt milk (about)

large cooking apples
caster sugar
oil for frying

Make the batter by mixing the dry ingredients and then beating in the egg and milk. A teaspoon of oil improves the consistency. Beat really well using a hand mixer or food processor, until bubbles form on the surface. Then set aside for at least an hour.

Prepare the apples by peeling and coring them and slicing them horizontally, into rings about ½" thick.

Heat enough oil in a large heavy pan to cover the bottom generously. When it is really hot dip the apple rings one at a time into flour and then into the batter. Fry over a hot fire for about 1 minute on each side, then reduce the heat and cook for a further 3 - 4 minutes on each side, turning once. As the fritters are cooked lift them out carefully with a slotted fish server or spoon and put them on kitchen paper to dry. Then transfer to a warm dish and dredge generously with caster sugar.

Serve hot.

Apple Cinnamon Fritters

4 medium sized apples (Orleans Reinette or Ribston Pippin)

1 lemon

4 Tbsp cider brandy (alt. dark rum or armagnac)

¼ l milk

5 Tbsp cider (alt. beer)

200 g flour

2 eggs

pinch of salt

oil for deep fat frying

1 Tbsp cinnamon

3 Tbsp vanilla sugar (see Tips & Tricks)

Mix flour, cider and milk in a bowl to form a thick dough (make sure not to produce any lumps). Now add the eggs with the salt and let rest for 30 min.

Meanwhile wash and peel and core the apples. Cut into slices of 1 cm thickness. Dowse with cider brandy and lemon juice cover and let stand.

Heat up a quantity of oil to 180°C in a saucepan sufficiently tall (only fill to a quarter!). Drip dry the apple slices and turn them lightly in some flour. Submerse slices individually in the dough, remove and let superfluous dough run back into the bowl. Only bake a few slices at a time, otherwise there is a risk that the oil will cool down too much, the oil might froth over or the slices may adhere to each other. Turn the slices over after about 2 minutes with a fork. Bake another 2 minutes and remove when golden-brown.

Mix vanilla sugar and cinnamon thoroughly in a soup bowl. Turn the individual fritters in the sugar mixture after they have been allowed to drain excess oil on some kitchen paper.

Spanish Apple Fritters

4 oz plain flour

2 Tbsp sugar

beer to mix (about pt)

3 large cooking apples (Howgate Wonder, Bramley or Lanes Prince Albert)

2 Tbsp sugar

cider brandy

cinnamon

dark brown sugar

Peel and core the apples and slice horizontally. Sprinkle with the sugar mixed with a pinch of cinnamon, and pour over the cider brandy. Leave to soak for several hours, or overnight.

Make batter by mixing the flour and the rest of the sugar and beating in enough beer to give a fairly thick smooth cream.

Melt some butter in a thick pan. Dip the drained apple slices in the batter and fry until golden brown on both sides. Drain, and turn in the dark brown sugar.

Serve hot with chilled whipped cream.

Apple Jacques

4 oz flour

1 egg

milk and water to mix - rather more than ¼ pt

1 tsp oil

3 - 4 dessert apples - Cox or Reinette

2 oz sugar

lemon juice

Make the batter in the usual way.

Prepare the apples by peeling, coring and slicing them, as if for a tart, not in rings. Sprinkle with sugar and lemon juice.

Heat a small frying pan until it is very hot, grease with oil or butter, and pour in a small amount of the pancake batter. Cover at once with a few slices of apple, followed by some more batter. Cook for about ½ minute or until the underside is brown, flip over and cook for another minute or so.

Serve the pancakes flat, sprinkled with sugar.

Harvest Pancakes

3 oz plain flour

1 egg

¼ pt milk

1 lb cooking apples (Lord Derby, Lanes Prince Albert or Belle de Boskoop)

1 heaped Tbsp brown sugar

2 - 3 cloves or a pinch of ground cloves

1 cup cider

2 Tbsp honey or syrup

1 oz raisins (not essential)

2 Tbsp cider brandy

Make batter by beating first the egg, then the milk into the flour until very smooth and slightly bubbly. Leave on one side for at least an hour. Prepare the filling by cooking the peeled, cored, sliced apples very gently in a tablespoon or two of water with sugar and cloves. Try to keep the fruit from turning to a puree, but it must be soft and with no surplus liquid.

For the sauce, warm together the cider and honey or syrup, with raisins if liked. Take off the flame and add the cider brandy.

Cook pancakes in the usual way. Fill each one with a generous spoonful of the apple mixture, roll up, and arrange in a dish. Pour over the sauce and serve very hot.

Apple and Lemon Croquettes

4 large cooking apples   fat for frying

6 Tbsp fine breadcrumbs

grated rind of one lemon

2 oz sugar

1 egg

crisp breadcrumbs

Bake the apples in their skins in the oven. While still hot, skin and mash them and add the soft breadcrumbs, lemon rind and sugar. Leave until cold and then make into rolls, 2 cm thick and 7 cm long.

Roll the croquettes in beaten egg and coat with crisp breadcrumbs. Fry until golden brown.

Serve hot with custard.

Apple Drop Scones

4 oz self-raising flour

½ tsp baking powder

pinch of salt

2 tsp caster sugar

1 crisp apple, peeled and grated

1 egg beaten in ¼ pt milk

Sieve flour, additional baking powder, salt and sugar. Beat in apple and the egg/milk mixture. Beat well for at least a minute, and cook at once by dropping spoonfuls onto a well-greased hot griddle or frying pan. Turn once during cooking. Cool the scones in a cloth on a wire tray, and wrap until ready to serve, preferably while still just warm, with butter.

Normandy Apple Batter

1½ lb crisp dessert apples (Ingrid Marie, Jester or Sunset)

butter for frying

4 oz sugar

small glass cider brandy

3 oz plain flour

3 eggs

½ pt milk

nutmeg or a little grated lemon rind

Peel, core and slice the apples and fry gently in the butter, keeping the slices whole. Transfer them to a flan dish or similar shallow oven-proof dish, and sprinkle with sugar. Swirl the cider brandy in the pan and pour the buttery mixture over the apples. Leave to soak for an hour or two.

To make the batter, beat the eggs into the milk with a spoonful of sugar and a pinch of salt. Add nutmeg or lemon rind and then gradually beat in the flour with a wooden spoon (or do the whole thing in a food processor).

Pour over the apples and bake for 1 hour at Mark 4/180°C.

Best served warm, sprinkled with icing sugar, with pouring cream.

Apple Dumplings

3 cooking apples

4 oz brown sugar

2 oz self-raising flour

2 oz oatmeal

¼ tsp salt

1 egg

¼ pt milk (approx)

1 oz butter

Peel, core and chop apples and mix with sugar.

Mix together the oatmeal, flour and salt and add the beaten egg and milk to make a drop batter. Stir in the melted butter.

Mix the apple with the batter, coating every piece. Grease some baking cups and fill with the mixture. Bake at Mark 5/190°C for about 30 minutes.

Serve hot with cream.

Witches Foam

3 large grenadier or bramley apples

5 oz sugar

2 egg whites

2 Tbsp smooth apricot jam

a little cider brandy or dark rum

Bake the apples in their skins until they are soft and foamy. Let them cool. When cold, remove the skins and turn the purée into a bowl. Stir in sugar, apricot jam, and liqueur if liked. Beat the egg whites until very stiff and fold them gently into the apple mixture. Serve piled up in glasses, well chilled.

Apple Amber

1 lb cooking apples (Grenadier or Bramley)

4 - 5 oz sugar

2 eggs

Peel and core the apples, cut them up and cook with about 3 oz sugar and a little water until they are reduced to a puree. Remove from the heat and fold in the beaten egg yolks. Turn the mixture into a suitable serving dish and bake at Mark 4/180°C for about 30 minutes.

Whisk the egg whites and fold in the rest of the sugar. Pile on top of the apples and put back into a cooling oven to brown the meringue. Serve hot.

To serve as a cold dish, give the meringue about an hour in a very cool oven, until it is set but not brown.

Orient Pudding

1 lb cooking apples (Bramley or Grenadier)
4 - 5 oz fresh white breadcrumbs
4 oz caster sugar
2 eggs
knob of butter

Peel, core and chop the apples and stew them with sugar to taste and a little water. Let the purée cool slightly.

Separate the eggs, and add the lightly beaten yolks, with the breadcrumbs and a knob of butter, to the apples. Turn the mixture into a soufflé dish.

Beat the egg whites and 1 oz sugar to stiff peaks.

Use this meringue to top the apple mixture.

Bake about 30 minutes at Mark 4/180°C.

Apple Meringue

6 cooking apples

½ cupful water

a little raspberry jam

pinch of ground cloves or cinnamon

1 Tbsp of sugar

2 egg whites

½ cupful sugar

Peel the apples, core and slice thinly. Place in a pan with water, sugar and cloves. Stew very gently until tender. Take from the pan and place in a small pie-dish. Allow to cool.

Whisk the egg whites briskly with the sugar until very stiff. Spread a little raspberry jam over the top of the apples. Pile the whisked egg white in heaps on top. Return to the oven for a minute or two to set and brown very slightly.

Serve cold.

Pommes a la Parisienne

6 good sized crisp dessert apples (James Grieve,   redcurrant jelly
Jester or Ribston Pippin)

4 oz vanilla sugar

½ pt water

3 eggs

2 oz sugar

2 oz ground almonds

Make a syrup with the vanilla sugar and water, and poach the peeled, cored apples in it, turning them over from time to time and being very careful not to break them.

When cooked but still firm lift them carefully out of the syrup and put on a wire rack until they are dry and cool.

Put them in a buttered fireproof dish and fill the cavities with redcurrant jelly.

Separate the eggs. Beat the yolks with the rest of the sugar until light and fluffy. Whip the egg whites until stiff, and fold them and the ground almonds into the beaten yolks. Pour the mixture over the apples, dust with a little vanilla sugar and bake for a few minutes in a fairly hot oven, Mark 6/200°C.

They should only need about 10 minutes, until the top is crisp and golden.

Serve warm (rather than hot).

Apple Mousse

1½ lb cooking apples

2 oz sugar

4 egg whites

2 Tbsp sugar

apricot or raspberry jam

liqueur - apricot brandy, grand marnier, kirsch

4 oz sugar for caramel

Bake the apples until quite soft. When they are cool enough to handle remove all the pulp and stir in about 2 oz sugar. Do not make the apples too sweet.

Melt 4 oz sugar with a spoonful of water over medium heat until it turns to caramel, stirring continuously. Use this caramel to coat the inside of a 2 pint mould. Leave it to harden.

Whip egg whites until stiff, fold in caster sugar and then fold the mixture into the apple sauce. Spoon the apple mixture into the mould and bake, standing in a pan of hot water, for about 1 hour at Mark 4/180°C. Allow to cool for about 15 minutes before turning out.

Heat the jam, thin if necessary with a little water, and sieve to remove pips if you are using raspberry jam. Flavour with liqueur, and serve the sauce hot.

Swiss Apple Gratin

1 lb cooking apples

3 oz sugar

3 - 4 oz zwieback (biscottes)

1 Tbsp sultanas

3 eggs

3 Tbsp sugar

3 Tbsp cream cheese thinned with a little milk

grated lemon rind

Peel and core the apples, cut them up and stew with the sugar and a little water until you have a smooth thick purée.

Crumble the Zwieback with a rolling pin or in a food processor until they are reduced to coarse crumbs.

Arrange layers of apple purée and Zwieback in a baking dish, finishing with a Zwieback layer. Beat egg yolks, sugar and cream cheese together until smooth. Add lemon rind, and pour the mixture over the apple and Zwieback.

Bake for about 20 minutes at Mark 4/180°C, until the custard is just set.

Apple Mincemeat Meringue

1½ lb cooking apples

4 oz sugar

grated lemon rind

pinch of cinnamon

knob of butter

½ lb mixed dried fruit

2 oz shelled chopped hazelnuts (or almonds)

2 large egg whites

4 oz caster sugar

Peel, core and chop the apples and stew them with sugar, lemon rind, a knob of butter and a little water. When quite soft and tender, beat to a purée. Add dried fruit (soaked for ½ hour in a little water, or cider, if it is very dry) and nuts. Put the mixture in a large soufflé dish, or divide between 6 small soufflé dishes.

Make meringue with egg whites and caster sugar, and cover the apple mixture with it. Put in a very cool oven for about 2 hours, until the meringue is set.

Serve cold, with pouring cream, or a custard made with the egg yolks.

Baked Apples

1 good sized cooking apple per person (Rev. Wilkes, Lord Derby or Orleans Reinette)

Demerara sugar - about 1 oz per apple

spices to taste

water

Core the apples but do not peel them. If they are very large, it helps them to cook more evenly and faster to draw a knife round the middle to break the skin. Fill the cores with sugar, mixed with a little grated lemon or orange peel and spices to taste - ground cloves, cinnamon, ginger.

Stand the apples in a baking dish which they fill without touching each other, pour in about ½ inch boiling water and bake in a moderate oven, Mark 4/180°C, until soft but not collapsing. Baste them with the juices occasionally.

Baked Apples with Sherry (Spanish)

6 large cooking apples (Howgate Wonder, Lord Derby or Lanes Prince Albert)

2 hard boiled eggs

1 tsp anisette

5 Tbsp medium sweet sherry

4 oz sugar

1 oz melted butter

Rinse apples under cold running water. Remove the cores, taking care not to cut deeply into flesh.

Separate the yolks from whites. Pound the yolks to a paste. Add the anisette and mix well. Add the sherry gradually, mixing well after each addition. Stir in sugar and melted butter.

Stand the apples in a shallow baking dish and fill the centre of each apple the mixture.

Bake in a hot oven (Mark 7/220°C) for 30 - 40 minutes. If the skins are too brown before they are cooked, lower heat after 30 minutes to Mark 5/190°C and bake for an extra 10 - 15 minutes.

Serve hot or cold.

Apple Whip

1 large can evaporated milk
1 pt apple purée
pinch ground cloves
pinch of coriander
finely grated rind of one lemon

Chill the milk and whip until thick and doubled in volume.

Blend in the purée, spices and lemon rind.

Pour into a serving dish and decorate with a little angelica or chopped cherry.

Serve chilled.

Buttered Apples

1 ½ lb cooking apples (Belle de Boskoop or Crispin)

4 oz butter

3 - 4 Tbsp sugar

6 slices white bread

⅓ pt whipped double cream

Peel apples and slice thickly. Melt 1 oz butter in a sauté pan and cook as many apple slices as will comfortably fit. Add 1 tablespoon of sugar and cook gently, turning until soft. Lift out with a slotted spatula and keep warm while you cook a second batch, adding more butter and sugar.

Remove the crusts from the bread and cut into rounds, allowing one per person.

When all the apples are done, add more butter to the pan and fry the bread on both sides.

Place the bread on a flat plate and spoon over the apple. Top each pile with whipped cream and serve immediately.

Apple Aspic

1½ lb cooking apples

4 - 6 oz white sugar

lemon juice and a little grated peel

1 Tbsp powdered gelatine dissolved in

¼ pt water

3 Tbsp cider brandy

glacé cherries

Peel, core and coarsely chop the apples and boil with very little water until soft. Purée with a blender and drive through a sieve. Sweeten to taste and stir in the cider brandy. You should have about a pint of purée.

Oil a 1 - 1¼ pint decorative mould, and arrange glace cherries, or other glacé fruits, over the bottom.

Add the dissolved gelatine to the apple purée and pour into mould. Leave to set and turn out when quite cold and firm.

Serve with a home-made custard sauce.

Apples Saint-Jean

1 apple per person (Jester, Sunset or Greensleeve)

sugar

butter

apricot or raspberry jam

crushed macaroons, about 1 Tbsp per apple

Core the apples and stuff them with sugar. Put a knob of butter on top of each apple, a few drops of water on each, cover the baking dish with thickly buttered paper and bake in a hot oven, Mark 6/200°C, until the apples are tender. Depending on the size and variety, this may take from 20 - 35 minutes. Remove the paper, spread a little jam over each apple (if using raspberry, or raspberry and redcurrant, sieve it first to get rid of the pips), and sprinkle the crushed macaroons over the jam. Put back into the oven for 5 minutes. Sprinkle the apples with a little cider brandy.

Serve hot.

Apple Gratin

3 tart apples

syrup (½ l water brought to the boil with ½ lb sugar)

1 Tbsp vanilla sugar

1 lb apple sauce

6 - 10 macaroons

5 Tbsp melted butter

Peel and core the apples.

Cut into quarters and poach in the syrup for 2 - 3 minutes, keeping them a little firm.

Strain and dry.

Arrange in an oven-proof dish on a layer of apple sauce.

Scatter some crushed macaroons on top.

Sprinkle with a little melted butter and brown the top in a slow oven.

Apple Jelly (dessert)

1 lb cooking apples

1 lemon jelly

2 oz sugar

¼ pt double cream

Peel, core and slice apples and cook with sugar in 3 tablespoons water - purée in mixer. Leave to cool.

Make jelly with ½ pint water. Cool.

Add to apple and lightly whisk in cream. Pour into mould to set.

Apple Ice Cream

¾ lb cooking apples, preferably Bramley

3 oz pale soft brown sugar, or 3 oz honey

pinch of cinnamon

1 tsp lemon juice

½ pt whipping cream (or ¼ pt single, ¼ pt double, stirred together)

Peel, core and chop the apples and cook in a tablespoon of water until you have a thick smooth purée. Stir in sugar or honey, cinnamon and lemon juice and leave to cool. Add a few drops of green colouring, if you like, or a spoonful of crab apple jelly, or even redcurrant jelly.

Whip the cream until it is just beginning to thicken, then stir in the cold apple purée and beat the mixture until it is really thick. Put into a plastic container, cover and freeze, stirring occasionally.

Like all fresh cream ices, this one will not retain its smooth texture for long (a month at most), as the water tends to separate out and form ice crystals. It is best made one or two days before it is to be eaten.

Apple Sorbet

500 g apples (Sunset, Fiesta or Kent)

500 g water

½ sachet gelatin

½ lemon (juice)

1 vanilla pod

Peel and core the apples. Coarsely grate quickly and mix with the lemon juice to prevent browning. Add apples and vanilla pod to the boiling water and continue to boil for 5 – 10 minutes. Remove the vanilla pod, take a few spoonfuls to dissolve the gelatine and puree the rest. Stir in the gelatine and mix thoroughly.

Let cool to room temperature and freeze, stirring occasionally.

Cider Sorbet

½ l cider

500 g sugar

4 egg whites

4 Tbsp cider brandy

Heat half of the cider and the sugar until all of the sugar is dissolved. Bring to the boil. Remove from the heat and let cool completely. Add the remainder of the cider and the cider brandy. Refrigerate. When the mixture is cold, place it in a large bowl, beat the egg whites until stiff (don't over beat though) and fold them into the mixture. Place in the freezer. After 30 minutes beat with a whisk. Beat again after a further 30 minutes. After another 30 minutes beat again. At this point the mixture is quite creamy and smooth and ready to serve.

Autumnal view across the valley

Cakes & Baking

"There was cakes and apples in all the Chapels . . ."

R H Barham

Dutch Apple Tart

1¼ lb dessert apples

2 oz sultanas

2 oz chopped blanched almonds

2 - 3 oz sugar

nutmeg

cinnamon

2 Tbsp apricot jam or redcurrant jam to glaze

8 oz shortcrust pastry

Line a 9" pie plate or flan dish with the pastry.

Peel, core and slice the apples and arrange them carefully on the pastry. They look prettiest in concentric circles.

Mix sultanas, almonds, 2 oz sugar and spices and sprinkle over the apples. Bake for 30 minutes at Mark 5/190°C.

While the tart is baking dissolve jam or jelly in a little water. Sieve and spread over the tart, sprinkle generously with sugar and put back into the oven for 2 - 3 minutes.

Serve cold but not chilled, with cream.

Tarte aux Pommes à L'alsacienne

125 g butter

75 g sugar

pinch of salt

250 g flour

125 mls strong cider (alt. white wine)

1 kg apples (Orleans Reinette, Ribston Pippin, Kent or Suntan)

1 handful of sugar to sprinkle over the apples

2 eggs

4 Tbsp vanilla sugar (see Tips & Tricks)

finely grated peel of 1 lemon

50 g sugar

250 mls cream

Stir butter and sugar until light and creamy. Add portions of flour alternating with portions of cider (just to avoid lumps).

Knead well and reserve in a cool place for 30 minutes.

Coat a greased 26 cm springform evenly with the dough and return to the cool place.

Now peel the apples, halve and remove the core. Score lengthwise on the outside.

Place the apple halves on the dough with their outside up.

Sprinkle some sugar over them and bake in a pre-heated oven for 30 minutes at Mark 5/225°C.

Meanwhile stir eggs, vanilla sugar, lemon peel and sugar until frothy. Stir in the cream and pour the mixture over the apples.

Return the cake to the oven for a further 10 minutes or until cooked and golden brown.

Apple Cake

175 g flour (if self-raising, dispense with the baking powder)

250 g sugar

3 eggs

3 - 4 Tbsp cream

1 tsp baking powder

2 Tbsp vanilla sugar (see Tips & Tricks)

salt

3 medium sized apples (Belle de Boskoop, Jester or Ingrid Marie)

2 handfuls of raisins

icing sugar

Carefully butter a 10" springform, and thinly coat with breadcrumbs or semolina.

Together with the sugar and the vanilla sugar beat the whole eggs and salt until creamy, then stir in the cream. Gradually add ¾ of the flour whilst stirring, avoiding lumps. Thoroughly mix the baking powder and the remaining flour and add to the dough. (The dough doesn't want to be to heavy and thick, it should slowly drip of a spoon). Peel and core the apples and cut into thin slices (4 – 5 mm). Pour the dough into the baking tin and place the apple slices in circles into the surface so that they are partly in the dough and partly overlapping each other.

Bake for 40 – 45 minutes in a pre-heated oven at 175°C.

After the cake has come out of the oven, slip a thin knife between cake and tin and follow it all the way round. This will loosen the side from the tin.

Let the cake rest for an hour, then remove it from the tin and dust it liberally with icing sugar.

Duvet Apple Cake This is a very tasty apple cake with a very light and fluffy topping (hence duvet)

140 g butter, 120 g sugar

2 Tbsp vanilla sugar, peel of 1 lemon

2 eggs

300 g flour, 3 tsp baking powder

125 ml milk

750 g apples (Prince Albert, Lord Derby or Belle de Boskoop)

50 g raisins

50 g sugar

cinnamon

3 eggs

80 g icing sugar

200 g cream

2 Tbsp vanilla sugar

Carefully butter a 10" springform, and thinly coat with breadcrumbs or semolina. Peel and core the apples and cut into thin slices. Beat sugar, vanilla sugar and butter in a bowl until they are creamy. Add the eggs one by one beating them in well, and last add the finely grated lemon peel. Gradually add small portions of alternately flour and milk to the mixture stirring well to avoid lumps. (Mix the last portion of flour with the baking powder prior to adding to the dough). Spread the dough into the tin and place the apple slices and raisins on top. Mix sugar and cinnamon in a little bowl and sprinkle generously over the apples. Bake in a preheated oven at 175°C for about 30 minutes. At that time whisk the whites of 3 eggs until the peaks will stand when the whisk is turned upside down. In a separate bowl whisk 3 egg-yolks, the icing sugar and the second lot of vanilla sugar until creamy, stir in the cream and fold under the egg-whites. Spread this mixture over the apple cake and return it to the oven for another 20 - 25 minutes until it is golden-brown.

Serve with lightly sweetened whipped cream or ice cream.

Spiced Apple Cheesecake

1 lb cream cheese

2 large cooking apples (Grenadier or Bramley's)

2 oz sultanas

3 oz sugar

pinch mixed spice and pinch cinnamon

1½ oz butter

4 oz digestive biscuits

2 ½ oz butter

Butter a 9" flan dish. To make the crust, melt about 2½ oz butter in a small pan and stir in 4 oz finely crumbled digestive biscuits. Spread the warm mixture over the base of the dish and pat down well. Leave to cool.

For the filling, peel core and slice the apples thinly, and cook them very gently in 1½ oz butter until they are quite soft but not reduced to mush. Add sultanas, sugar and spice to taste.

Put the cheese in a large bowl and whip lightly. Smoothen, if necessary, with a few drops of milk. Stir in the soft apples while they are still warm. Check the flavour, adding a little lemon juice if the mixture is too sweet or bland, and pile the filling onto the biscuit base. Chill well.

(Try brushing the base with a little melted plain chocolate before adding the topping).

Apple Torte

4 oz butter

4 oz sugar

2 eggs

6 oz self-raising flour

1 lb cooking apples

4 oz chopped walnuts

½ tsp powdered mace

1 Tbsp cider brandy

Cream the butter and sugar until light and fluffy. Mix in the beaten eggs and flour alternately.

Peel, core and slice the apples and add to the mixture, together with the walnuts, mace and cider brandy.

Mix all well together and then turn into a buttered square baking tin.

Bake in a moderate oven, Mark 4/180°C for 45 minutes.

Serve with whipped cream laced with a little brandy.

Apple Gingerbread

1 lb cooking apples

12 oz self-raising flour

2 tsp ground ginger

6 oz butter

5 oz soft brown sugar

3 oz golden syrup

3 oz black treacle

2 eggs

For this cake you need an 8" square tin, greased and lined with paper.

Wash the apples but do not peel them, and grate them up or chop finely in a food processor. Sprinkle with a few drops of lemon juice to stop them turning brown.

Heat sugar, butter, golden syrup and treacle until the sugar is dissolved. Sift flour and ginger into a mixing bowl. Beat the eggs and add to the flour, together with the melted ingredients. Beat until smooth, then stir in the apples.

Spoon into the prepared tin and smooth over the top.

Bake at Mark 5/190°C for about 1 - 1¼ hours, until a skewer comes out clean. Allow to cool in the tin for ten minutes before turning out. Dust a little caster sugar over the top.

Very good as it is, it can be made into more of a party cake by lemon or orange icing.

Apple Upside-Down Cake

1 lb cooking apples (Lord Derby)

6 oz self-raising flour

3 oz soft light brown sugar

3 oz sugar

2 oz butter

1 egg

1 tsp mixed spice

milk

Use a 7 - 8" cake tin, well buttered but not lined. Peel and core the apples and cut them into neat slices. Arrange in the bottom of the tin, and cover with the brown sugar mixed with the spices.

Rub the butter into the flour and add the sugar. Mix with a lightly beaten egg and enough milk to make a firm dough. Spread this over the apples.

Bake at Mark 6/200°C for 35-40 minutes. Allow to cool in the tin for a few minutes, and then turn out onto a serving dish.

Serve warm, with cold cream or ice cream.

Apple and Lemon Cake

5 oz self-raising flour

3 oz butter

3 oz caster sugar

1 egg & 1 egg yolk

1 large cooking apple

1 small red-skinned dessert apple (Katy or Ingrid Marie)

½ l water

½ lb sugar

2 oz soft brown sugar

2 oz lemon curd

Cream butter and sugar until light and fluffy, then beat in egg plus additional yolk. Fold in the sifted flour.

Spoon into a 8" round cake tin, greased and floured, and bake at Mark 5/190°C for about 30 minutes, until pale golden brown. Cool on a wire rack.

Core the dessert apple, preserving the skin, and cut into thin slices. Blanche the slices in syrup (made of ½ l water and ½ lb sugar brought to the boil) for 2 minutes. Drain well.

Peel, core and chop the cooking apple and stew it gently with the brown sugar and a tablespoon of water until thick and soft. Puree in a food processor or using a blender. Pass through a sieve and mix with the lemon curd. Spread this mixture over the cake. Decorate with slices of the dessert apple, and serve at once.

Apple Bread

12 oz plain flour, white, or mixed white and wholemeal

1 tsp baking powder

½ tsp bicarbonate of soda

½ tsp salt

2 - 3 eating apples

2 oz chopped walnuts or chopped mixed nuts

3 oz grated wensleydale cheese

5 oz soft light brown sugar

2 oz butter

2 eggs

Core the apples but do not peel them. Chop finely in a food processor, or use a coarse grater. Keep as much juice as you can.

Cream butter and sugar. Add the eggs one at a time, beating after each addition. Stir in the chopped apples and juice, cheese and nuts.

Mix all the dry ingredients together and fold into the creamed mixture. Be careful not to over mix.

Bake in a well-greased loaf tin at Mark 5/190°C for about an hour. Test with a skewer. Cool on a rack, and do not store in a tin until it is absolutely cold, or the apples may turn mouldy.

Eat just sliced and buttered (or with some more cheese sandwiched between two slices as a perfect picnic food). A few sultanas may be added as well as, or instead of, the nuts.

Apple Muffins

8 oz plain flour

1 tsp baking powder

8 oz lard

1 lb cooking apples

1 egg

2 oz black treacle

Sift together flour and baking powder. Rub in the lard.

Peel, core, and chop or grate the apples. Beat the egg. Make a well in the flour mixture and stir in apples, egg and treacle. Stir until you have a stiff, sticky dough.

Spread the dough on a well-greased baking tray in a hot oven, Mark 8/230°C, for about 25 minutes or until golden brown. While still hot, cut into rounds, or more economically into squares, and cool these on a rack. Serve while still just warm, split open, buttered and dusted with caster sugar, which may be flavoured with cloves, cinnamon or ginger to taste.

Apple and Raisin Loaf

8 oz self-raising flour

pinch of salt

2 oz butter

2 oz seedless raisins

grated lemon rind

2 - 3 oz soft brown sugar

½ lb cooking apples, chopped finely or grated

1 egg

milk

Mix flour and salt and rub in the butter. Add raisins, lemon rind, sugar and chopped apples. Leave the skins on unless they are very tough. Beat egg with 4 tablespoons milk and add to the dry mix.

(The dough should be firm but not too stiff. The quantity of milk required depends on the juiciness of the apples, and you may need to add another spoonful or two).

Bake in a small loaf tin, well greased, at Mark 5/190°C for about 40 minutes.

Allow to cool completely before storing in a tin.

Best eaten when fresh.

Early morning mist

Miscellaneous

". . . it is even congenial for monks to have the care of a garden, to till the land, and to take interest in a good crop of apples."

Cassiodorus - Institutes

Sweet-Sour Red Cabbage

1 small red cabbage (about 2 lbs)

2 medium onions

3 Tbsp butter

2 cooking apples (Belle de Boskoop, Orleans Reinette or Crispin)

2 Tbsp sugar

1 glass cider

2 Tbsp port or sweet dessert wine (madeira, sherry, marsala)

2 Tbsp cider vinegar

1 bay leave

salt & pepper

Slice the cabbage thinly. Slice the onions and peel, core and slice the apples. In an oven-proof casserole sweat the onions in the melted butter. Add the cabbage and sweat for a few minutes. Add the cider and season with salt and pepper. Cook with the lid on for 15 minutes. Stir in the apples, add the bay leave and transfer to the oven. (If the lid is not tight-fitting, it is a good idea to cover with foil first).

Cook for about 2½ hours in a slow oven, gas Mark 2/150°C.

It improves with reheating.

Excellent with pork, goose, hare, and sausages.

Apple Sauce

1 ½ lb cooking apples

water

2 tsp brown sugar

salt & pepper

Peel, core and coarsely chop the apples. Put into a heavy pan with a tablespoon of water and cook until soft, stirring occasionally to prevent burning. Flavour with brown sugar, salt and pepper.

These quantities should make a good pint of sauce - people always seem to eat the lot!

The flavouring may be varied by adding a couple of cloves to the apples while they are cooking (be sure to remove them before serving), or by substituting 2 tablespoons redcurrant jelly for the brown sugar.

Apple Sauce with Orange

1½ lb cooking apples

grated rind and juice of one small orange

1 oz butter

1 - 2 Tbsp brown sugar

Peel, core and coarsely chop the apples. Put into a heavy pan with a tablespoon of water and cook until soft, stirring occasionally to prevent burning. Add the grated orange rind and juice. When the apples are reduced to a puree add sugar to taste, and a pinch of salt if you like. At the last moment stir the butter into the hot sauce until it is just dissolved.

Also good with lemon instead of orange, but go easy on the juice.

Apple and Quince Sauce

1 quince

4 small apples

½ pt cider

3 oz sugar

1 oz butter

Peel, core and coarsely grate the fruit.

Put the grated quince in a small saucepan, pour in the cider and bring to the boil. Simmer for 10 minutes until tender.

Add the apple and simmer for 10 minutes longer. Stir well with a wooden spoon to make a thickish pulp.

Add the sugar and cook gently until melted. Stir well and add the butter.

Ideal with roast pork or goose.

Apple and Horseradish Sauce

1 lb apples
2 oz ground almonds
1 Tbsp sugar
3 Tbsp freshly grated horseradish
salt
lemon juice or vinegar

Core the apples and bake in the oven. Skin them and pass them through a sieve.

Stir in the sugar and a little salt. Add enough lemon juice or vinegar to make it smooth.

Add the almonds and lastly the horseradish.

Taste for seasoning. The sauce should be sweet-sour.

Serve cold.

Apple and Onion Stuffing

3 large cooking apples (Lord Derby or
Howgate Wonder)

4 large onions

8 oz cooked potatoes

½ tsp dried sage

½ tsp grated lemon rind

pinch of thyme

salt & pepper

Peel and core the apples and chop very finely.

Chop the onion and cook for 5 minutes to soften a little.

Mash the potatoes.

Mix all the ingredients together and season well.

Use to stuff goose, duck or pork.

Nutty Apple Stuffing

3 sticks celery
1 green apple
3 oz chopped nuts
1 large carrot
2 oz butter
2 tsp mixed herbs

Purée the celery, apple and carrot.

Melt the butter in saucepan. Remove from heat and add the other ingredients, mixing well.

Season well and use to stuff breast of lamb, duck, goose, or the neck end of a turkey.

Apples Baked with Cream Cheese

8 eating apples (Greensleeves, Jester or Ribston Pippin)

250 g cream cheese

red currant jelly

Core and peel the apples, keeping them whole. Smoothen up the cream cheese with a few drops of cream, season lightly with salt and pepper and a scrap of grated orange or lemon peel if you like it. Stuff the apples with the cream cheese. Dip into melted redcurrant jelly, and bake in a medium oven until soft. Allow to cool, and brush with more redcurrant jelly.

Delicious with ham, gammon, roast pork and game.

Yoghurt and Apple Dressing

5 oz plain yoghurt

2 Tbsp apple juice

good pinch ground ginger

good pinch ground cardamom or cinnamon

salt

Add the apple juice gradually to the yoghurt. Stir in the spices and a little salt to taste.

Apple Water Ice

1 lb cooking apples
3 oz sugar lemon juice
1 large egg white

Peel, core and slice the apples and cook in a little water until quite soft. Pass through a fine sieve of a jelly bag - the liquid should be quite clear. You should have about ¾ pint liquid; if necessary add a little more water. Bring to the boil and add about 3 oz sugar. Boil for 5 minutes and leave to cool. Stir in a little lemon juice.

Whip the egg white until stiff, and fold in the apple syrup. Freeze, stirring occasionally.

This ice can be flavoured with mint; put a couple of sprigs of mint into a little muslin bag, bang it with the back of a spoon to crush the leaves, and put it into the clear liquid while it is boiling up with the sugar.

An ice to serve with a dish of game.

Apple Jelly (preserve)

Windfall apples or Crab apples
preserving sugar
water

Wash the fruit and cut into rough pieces, without peeling or removing the pips. Put into a large pan, cover with water and simmer until the fruit is soft. Strain through a jelly bag into a large basin. If you haven't got a jelly bag, use a closely woven white cloth such as an old pillowcase draped over a colander. Whichever method you use, do not hurry the straining process, and do not be tempted to squeeze the bag or cloth at the end or the jelly will be cloudy.

Measure the juice and use 1 lb sugar to each pint. Boil until setting point is reached, pot and cover.

Crab apples are best used on their own, but if you like you can flavour ordinary cooking apples with a quince or two.

Spiced Apple Butter

4 lb cooking apples

1½ lb sugar

1¼ pt cider

juice of 1 lemon

cloves and a piece of cinnamon stick tied up in a muslin bag

Peel but do not core the apples and slice them up roughly. Put in a pan with water, lemon juice and spices and cook until the apples are a soft pulp. Remove bag of spices and blend thoroughly with a hand-blender or food processor and sieve.

Return the purée to the pan, add the sugar and reheat slowly, stirring to make sure the sugar is fully dissolved. When it is, bring to the boil and cook until the mixture is really thick, stirring frequently.

Pot and cover.

Use as a spread for toasted bread.

Apple and Tomato Chutney

3 lb tomatoes

3 lb apples

1 lb onions

1 green pepper

8 oz sultanas

¼ oz root ginger, finely grated

2 pt spiced vinegar

8 oz soft brown sugar

1 level tsp salt

8-10 red chillies

Skin the tomatoes, peel and core the apples, peel the onions and wash the pepper. Chop finely and mince together.

Place in a pan with the sultanas, the ginger, vinegar, sugar and salt. Tie the chillies loosely in a muslin bag and add to the pan. Bring to the boil, stirring until the sugar has dissolved.

Simmer uncovered until the vegetables are soft and the contents of the pan reduced and thickened.

Remove the muslin bag. Pour the hot chutney into hot clean jars and seal.

Besides being very tasty, this recipe is a good opportunity to use up left over apples and windfalls. (They should be hearty and mustn't be too ripe!)

Apple and Date Preserve

4 lb cooking apples

4 lb sugar

1 lb stoned dates

grated rind and juice of 3 lemons

3 Tbsp finely grated stem ginger

cinnamon stick tied up in a muslin bag

Peel and chop the apples and put them in a large bowl with the lemon juice. Cover with sugar and leave overnight. Next day transfer to a large pan and stir over low heat until all the sugar is dissolved. Add chopped dates and lemon rind, ginger and cinnamon bag. Bring to the boil.

Cook for about 25 minutes, until setting point is reached. Remove spice bag, pot and cover.

Mincemeat

1½ lb cooking apples (Howgate Wonder, Belle de Boskoop, Orleans Reinette)

¾ lb raisins

¾ lb currants

¾ lb sultanas

¼ lb mixed peel

2 oz chopped blanched almonds

¾ lb suet

¾ lb soft brown sugar or molasses

sugar grated

nutmeg, cinnamon, mace (about ½ tsp each)

grated rind and juice of 1 lemon and 1 orange

4 Tbsp cider brandy or rum

Peel, core and chop the apples into small pieces. Mix all the ingredients together, stirring well. Add the brandy or rum last. Pack tightly into jars, preferably glass preserving jars with clip-on or screw tops. If you have to use jam jars, seal them as tightly as possible with several layers of greaseproof paper tied on firmly.

Should keep for several years and improve with keeping.

Granny's Chutney (uncooked)

1 lb onions

2 lb cooking apples

2 lb seedless raisins

2 lb sugar

3 pt vinegar (preferably cider or white wine)

1½ oz ground ginger

2 oz salt

¼ lb mustard seed, lightly crushed

Bring the vinegar to the boil and add ginger and salt.

Chop apples and onions finely. Put them in a large bowl, and stir in raisins, sugar and mustard seed. Pour over the boiling vinegar mixture and stir well.

This uncooked chutney should be kept for at least a month before eating. It needs stirring frequently, once a day if possible. Either leave it in the mixing bowl, with a foil lid, or put it into jars, leaving enough room to stir.

Apple and Apricot Jam

1 lb dried apricots

12 lb apples (any windfall will do)

sugar

water

Cut apricots into pieces and soak in as much water as they will absorb.

Wash and cut up the apples without peeling. Boil in a little water until soft. Pass the fruit through a sieve. Add the apricots and weigh.

Bring the fruit to the boil. To each pound of pulp allow ¾ lb sugar (or 1 lb sugar to 1 pint of pulp). Boil quickly to setting point. Stir well and bottle.

(The faster the fruit boils, the deeper the colour and the stronger the flavour of the jam).

Apple Chutney

2 lb cooking apples

¾ lb onions

1 lb sugar

3 tsp salt

1¼ pt vinegar

½ tsp cayenne pepper

4 oz sultanas

2 oz crystallised ginger, chopped

1 clove garlic

Peel and core the apples and chop into 1 cm dice. Skin and mince the onions.

Put all the ingredients into a pan and simmer very slowly. Stir often and do not cover the pan.

Cook for 2 ½ hours until chutney is thick and has no free vinegar on the surface.

Pour into hot clean jars and seal.

Apple Curd

2 lb cooking apples

2 eggs

8 oz unsalted butter

8 oz sugar

juice of 1 lemon

Peel, core and chop the apples and stew them in a little water until they are soft. Puree with a blender and sieve. Add sugar and melted butter, then beat in the eggs and cook slowly for about 30 minutes, preferably over hot water to ensure that the mixture does not curdle or turn into scrambled eggs.

When it is thick and creamy, add lemon juice, pot and cover.

Dried Apples

One excellent way of preserving apples is to dry them.

Any apples are suitable as long as they are sound and not over-ripe. (Cookers are quite tart even when dried and are best used chopped up in muesli or reconstituted in compote or sauce).

Peel, core and slice the apples into 5 mm thick rounds (drop them into a bowl of water to which you have added the juice of a lemon as you prepare them, to stop them discolouring). When you have prepared a batch for drying, pat them dry and either lay them out on baking trays or string them and fasten the strings to the oven shelves. Dry in a very cool oven, not more than 70°C. They may take 12 hours or more; if in doubt, allow them to cool off, check for moisture and if necessary give them another few hours.

Alternatively you can fasten the strings on a suitable frame (or from wall to wall) in a warm and well ventilated room.

When dried completely they may be stored in boxes, but do be sure to check the boxes once in a while in case there is still the odd damp one that will start to go mouldy.

Chopped dried apples are an excellent addition to muesli. Chopped and then soaked they may be used instead of fresh chopped apples in many of the recipes in this book. To cook them, simmer very gently until they are soft and sweeten to taste. Good for apple sauces and spicy apple puddings.

Muesli

1 heaped Tbsp mixed grains   *water*

½ apple, grated

1 tsp honey

*raisins and nuts to taste (hazel nuts are the
classic addition, but almonds or walnut pieces
are also very good)*

lemon or orange juice

The grains should be mixed with a little water and left for a few minutes until they are slightly soft but not soggy. Sometimes it is suggested to leave them overnight, but this tends to destroy the crunchy texture that is part of the attraction of muesli.

Mix in the other ingredients, and serve with milk to taste.

Apple Muesli with Yoghurt

2 dessert apples

2 Tbsp honey

½ pt natural (unsweetened) yoghurt

2 Tbsp lemon juice

4 oz mixed grains (can be bought in most health food stores or supermarkets)

Core the apples, leaving the peel on them, and chop finely. Pour lemon juice over them. Add yoghurt and honey, and a little water if the mixture is very thick. Stir in the grains and allow to stand for a few minutes. Turn the mixture into a serving dish and sprinkle with some nuts, if liked, and a little demerara sugar.

Crab-Apple Wine

4 lb or more Crab apples

8 pt boiling water

wine-makers yeast

juice of 1 lemon (optional)

3 lb sugar

Roughly chop up apples - cores, stalks and all - into a pail or large bowl. Vessel must be pottery or plastic or stainless steel.

Pour on boiling water, stir well.

Leave to stand for four days, stirring well daily, crushing the apples to get out as much juice as possible.

Strain off the juice onto sugar, add yeast and lemon juice if liked and put into fermenting vessel.

Leave to ferment in a fairly warm atmosphere - kitchen ideal (may be vigorous at first, so watch it).

Rack when quieted down, at least once.

Bottle when clear.

Try to resist at least for six months before opening.

Toffee Apples

12 medium-sized dessert apples (sunset, fiesta   ¼ pt water
or greensleeve)

12 wooden skewers

6 oz golden syrup

12 oz soft brown sugar

1 oz butter

1 tsp cider vinegar

Wash and dry the apples, remove their stalks and push a wooden skewer firmly into each one.

Put remaining ingredients into a heavy saucepan and heat gently, stirring continuously, until the sugar is dissolved. Then bring to the boil and boil rapidly to 145°C (290°F), or until a drop in cold water sets hard and snaps cleanly.

Dip apples in the toffee one by one, twisting them about to ensure they are completely covered. Immediately dip in iced water, and then stand on a buttered baking tray to set.

NB Dipping and cooling need to be done very fast:

It helps to have an assistant. The apples should be wrapped in waxed paper if they are not to be eaten at once, to preserve the crispness of the coating.

Oat Crisp

8 oz quick cooking oats

4 Tbsp Demerara sugar

3 oz butter, preferably unsalted

This recipe does not contain any apples, but it is very useful for preparing apple dishes such as crumbles, baked apples and open apple tarts.

Melt the butter slowly in a large saucepan. Do not let it fizzle and boil. Stir in the other ingredients. Sprinkle the mixture over the bottom of a large shallow tin, such as a swiss roll tin (ungreased). Cook for about 10 minutes at 165°C, Mark 4, stirring once or twice to break up any lumps.

Leave to cool. When quite cold crush with a fork, or put between two sheets of greaseproof paper and run a rolling pin over it until the mixture is like coarse crumbs. Store in an airtight jar. Keeps well in a cool dry place.

Apple Ointment (a Tudor recipe)

1 lb flead

1 lb apples

1 oz cloves

½ pt olive oil

½ pt rosewater

juice of 2 lemons and grated lemon peel

Slice the flead and put it into an earthenware pippin with the lemon peel and cloves. Add the apples, coarsely chopped, peel, cores and all.

Cook in a very slow oven for about 3 hours, or in a slow cooker for 10 - 12 hours.

Strain the melted fatty liquid through several layers of fine muslin, add oil, lemon juice and rosewater and stir well. Leave it to stand for a few hours and then pour into jars.

Flead, the very fine, pure lard obtained from the inner membrane of the pig's body, may be difficult to obtain even from a country butcher unless he has his own slaughterhouse. The next best thing is lard prepared by a butcher. Melt it very gently and skim off any impurities before adding the chopped apples and lemon peel.

The autumn haze turns it into a magical valley

Tips & Tricks

"I am convinced digestion is the great secret of life"

Sydney Smith

Suet Pastry

To make a suet pastry: first mix the twice the amount dry self-raising flour with the suet in a large bowl using the blade of a knife. Gradually add water drop-wise mixing the mixture with the knife until it becomes quite sticky. Now continue bringing then dough further together using your hands, kneading it until it is quite elastic and springy, leaving the bowl clean. (Add more water if it appears too dry or dusty, but let it remain quite firm).

How to steam a pudding

You can either steam a pudding enveloped in a well floured large smooth cotton cloth (a pudding cloth) or in a well greased pudding basin lined with grease prove paper.

The pudding basin should have a good lid and must be closed water-tight to keep water and steam out. During cooking it is essential to keep the water boiling all the time, particularly if you use a pudding cloth, otherwise it will go soggy. (If you have to add more water, bring it to the in a kettle first).

All steamed puddings, with or without suet, cook beautifully in a slow cooker. They don't dry out and they don't fill the kitchen with steam. Follow the timing given in a slow cooker recipe book, remembering that is almost impossible to overcook anything.

How to test that a cake or pudding is cooked

Insert the blade of a slender knife (or better still a skewer) into the cake or pudding and withdraw: if it is well cooked it will come out clean. If there is dough clinging to it, some more cooking is required.

How to make really smooth soup or puree

The easiest way of getting soups and purees to be really smooth is by blending them thoroughly with a hand blender or a food processor. The trick is to pass it through a sieve afterwards to remove those persistently hard bits that have evaded the blending knives.

Vanilla sugar

Fill a 2 pint kilner jar (or any other jar with a tight fitting lid) ¾ with sugar. Take two vanilla pods cut lengthwise and place in the sugar. Close the lid tightly and shake the jar once a week. The pod can stay or it can be removed after about 4 weeks.

If you need vanilla sugar urgently put 2 tablespoons of sugar into a small jar with a tight fitting lid and add 2 drops of vanilla extract. Shake thoroughly.

Freezing ice-cream and sorbets

The most elegant way here is to use a standalone ice-cream maker. Alternatively you can use those that use a bowl that is cooled for a few hours beforehand in a freezer (there are some that are placed entirely in the freezer with a thin cable coming out).

If you haven't got any of this you can still make perfectly good ice-cream and sorbets:

Place the ice mixture in your fridge to cool it as low as possible before you start. (This may be done overnight). Now take a large metal bowl (metal conduct heat better than ceramics or glass) and place it in the freezer for 10 – 15 minutes. Handle the bowl only at its brim (you don't want to heat it up with your hands). Place your ice mixture in the bowl and return to the freezer. Initially return to the freezer every 30 minutes to give the mixture a good stir. (Take the bowl out of the freezer for as short a period as possible). When the mixture starts to set on the bowl scrape it with a long handled scraper more frequently until the whole is frozen but still creamy.

The addition of gelatine to sorbets help to freeze it more smoothly and stops it from separating when stored after freezing.

Tree Care

The domesticated apple which we enjoy so much for eating and cooking, has its origins on the slopes of the Tien Shen mountains situated in the North of the Himalayas. Growing as a sizeable tree high up on mountain slopes in the centre of Northern Asia, it is not only used to the hot summers and cold winters of a continental climate but also to warm autumn days with cool nights and plenty of precipitation without exposure to stagnant damp - quite different from the climate of Yorkshire. This does not mean that apple trees could not survive in Yorkshire; they do so quite well. However, life here presents a constant struggle for them. Susceptibility to disease, pests, soil condition and positioning is therefore more pronounced and requires careful consideration.

Tree care already starts before planting. To give the tree as much help as possible to grow well and produce abundant good fruit, the first consideration should be where to place it. In order for wild bees and other beneficial insects to help pollination and keep pests at bay, the tree should, ideally, be in company with other trees, bushes and shrubs without being too close to them. (However, care must be taken that nearby trees are not of a kind that is likely to overshadow the little apple tree). The position should, of course, be sunny most of the day. Air should move around it freely, but it must be sheltered from rough winds. The soil does not need to be too rich but there has to be a good supply of water throughout the year and the ground must be well drained: apple trees don't like "wet feet".

Although apple trees can be grown from pips, the propagation of a particularly good example that we may have found and come to love can only easily be done by grafting parts of the variety we like onto a "root-stock". This means that the fruiting part of the new tree is genetically identical with the parent tree and should yield similar fruit. The careful choice of this rootstock (whether "dwarfing" or "vigorous") allows apple trees to be planted in gardens of almost any size, as the rootstock will to a large degree determine how fast and big a tree will grow.

Because grafting is yet another insult to it, it is necessary to give the tree some more help. This, at least for the dwarf trees, can be provided initially by a stake planted firmly in the ground and fastened gently to its trunk. This will give support particularly when there is a heavy crop. The stake may be needed for the whole lifetime of the tree and since dead wood eventually rots away, it may need to be replaced after some five or ten years.

Nutrients in the soil are normally replenished through the surface. This means that plants growing closely together will compete for nutrients and moisture. Water transporting the nutrients through the soil will by-pass the not yet fully developed root system of a newly planted tree. The situation will be worse if there are plenty of other roots around soaking it all up. It will help the tree for the first few years if competition is reduced by keeping bare an area around its stem. This area should have the diameter of the tree's crown since this reflects the approximate extension of its roots.

When it comes to feeding it pays to remember that the roots grow outwards as well as downwards; and it is the newly grown root that can take up most nutrients. Fertiliser or manure applied close to the stem is hardly absorbed, but if applied in a circle under the outer third of the crown it will feed the tree well, unless it is swallowed up by too many weeds or grass growing there.

Since apple trees grown in Yorkshire will turn out smaller than those in their original habitat because of the differences in climate, the branches will be rather closer together than is helpful for the production of a good crop. In addition most trees are also expected to look nice. This is where careful pruning comes in. Its aim is to remove just enough of the branches to allow the tree to develop the desired shape and also to expose the maximum of its foliage to the sun. The leaves produce many of the sugars and substances that are eventually found in the apples. They can only do that if they receive enough sunlight to carry out photosynthesis. Consequently a nice branch with good flowers on it cannot do much for the development of their fruit if it is permanently overshadowed by other branches.

Which branches to shorten or cut out and where to cut exactly will depend very much on the individual situation. However, branches that grow more horizontally from the trunk are usually stronger and therefore more worthwhile keeping. Branches that rub against each other will be damaged; one of them should be removed. Branches closer to the top of the tree should be shorter, otherwise they will always cast a shadow on the lower ones. Finally, particularly in the small garden, it is a good idea to keep the lowest branches far enough off the ground to facilitate the clearing of weeds, mowing the lawn, etc.

All this might sound rather laborious and daunting. Don't forget though, you planted your tree mainly to enjoy it. Most of the work will be spread out over the year and a little work done regularly goes a long way without being too demanding.

Index

Apple Almond Pudding	64	Apple Cinnamon Fritters	71
Apple Amber	80	Apple Curd	132
Apple and Apricot Jam	130	Apple Drop Scones	76
Apple and Chestnut Soup	13	Apple Dumplings	78
Apple and Date Crumble	61	Apple Fritters	70
Apple and Date Preserve	127	Apple Gingerbread	106
Apple and Grape Clafoutis	65	Apple Gratin	93
Apple and Horseradish Sauce	118	Apple Ice Cream	95
Apple and Lemon Cake	108	Apple Jacques	73
Apple and Lemon Croquettes	75	Apple Jelly (dessert)	94
Apple and Nut Salad	17	Apple Jelly (preserve)	124
Apple and Onion Stuffing	119	Apple Meringue	82
Apple and Quince Sauce	117	Apple Mince Pie	45
Apple and Raisin Loaf	111	Apple Mincemeat Meringue	86
Apple and Raisin Slaw	18	Apple Mousse	84
Apple and Tomato Chutney	126	Apple Muesli with Yoghurt	135
Apple Aspic	91	Apple Muffins	110
Apple Bread	109	Apple Oat Crumble	60
Apple Burger with a Curry Dip	37	Apple Ointment (a Tudor recipe)	139
Apple Cake	102	Apple Pan Dowdy	63
Apple Charlotte	62	Apple Raisin Pudding	56
Apple Chutney	131	Apple Roll	59

Index

Apple Roly Poly	53	Cider Sorbet	97
Apple Sauce	115	Cousin Polly's Pudding	55
Apple Sauce with Orange	116	Crab-Apple Wine	136
Apple Sorbet	96	Cucumber and Apple Soup	14
Apple Soup	12	Danish Apple and Chocolate Pudding	67
Apple Streusel Pie	48	Deep Dish Apple Pie	42
Apple Strudel	50	Dorset Apple Cake	51
Apple Torte	105	Dried Apples	133
Apple Upside-Down Cake	107	Dutch Apple Tart	100
Apple Water Ice	123	Duvet Apple Cake	103
Apple Whip	89	Escalopes of Veal with Apple	27
Apple, Celery and Turkey Salad	20	Eve's Pudding	52
Apples Baked with Cream Cheese	121	Freezing ice-cream and sorbets	144
Apples Saint-Jean	92	French Apple Tart	47
Australian Summer Salad	23	Fried Apple and Cheese Sandwich	31
Bacon and Apple Salad	21	Gammon with Marmalade and Apple Glaze	32
Baked Apples	87	Garrion Apple Pie	46
Baked Apples with Sherry (Spanish)	88	Granny's Chutney (uncooked)	129
Beetroot and Apple Salad	19	Grasmere Apple Gingerbread	68
Brown Betty	58	Grilled Pork Chops with Cider Sauce	30
Buttered Apples	90	Harvest Pancakes	74
Cheese and Apple Salad	22	Himmel und Erde	29